# GARDENING
# THE HEART

# GARDENING THE HEART

*40 Devotions For Thoughtful Women*

Joyce E. Bellous

CLEMENTS PUBLISHING
Toronto, Ontario

Published 2005 by
CLEMENTS PUBLISHING
6021 Yonge Street, Box 213
Toronto, Ontario M2M 3W2 Canada
www.clementspublishing.com

Cover design by Greg Devitt <www.gdevitt.com>

Library and Archives Canada Cataloguing in Publication

Bellous, Joyce Edith, 1948–
Gardening the Heart / Joyce E. Bellous.

ISBN 1-894667-77-8

1. Christian women—Religious life. 2. Christian life—Baptist authors.
I. Title.

BV4844.B44 2005      242'.643      C2005-901471-7

*Dedication*

*To the women who gathered in the spring of 2002,
at Canmore, Alberta, in the Rocky Mountains,
especially Irene Sotropa and Mayvis Goranson*

# CONTENTS

# PREFACE

The purpose of this book of devotions is to strengthen our love for God. It is a Christian practice to set aside forty days for focused spiritual reflection, so one way to use this book is to read one devotion per day until you read them all.

The short story expresses a theme that runs through all the devotions. You may choose to read the short story first, or in the middle (as you find it in the book) or at the end of your reading.

The book is also divided into sections, so you might take an extended period of time and read a group of devotions in one sitting and so cover the book on four different occasions. However you choose to read these devotions, my prayer is that they will move you to realize more fully how much you are loved by God.

In writing this book I owe a debt to the women who have nutured, suported and challenged me. In paticular, I am grateful to my three mothers: Dorothy Sears, Nettie Bellous, and Evelina Orteza y Miranda.

I also want thank Pat Webb, Leanne Friesen and Karen Elliott for reading the manuscript and for providing insightful comments.

# EVERY MORNING HAS A MIRROR IN IT

## DEVOTIONS 1-10

# 1

# EVERY MORNING
# HAS A MIRROR IN IT

*James 1:23-25*

It is safe to assume you looked in a mirror this morning. Can you recapture the look on your face as you saw your image in the glass? Close your eyes. Recall your expression. Do you picture your face? My mother used to say: Spend as much time in front of the mirror as you need, and do your best. Then, walk out the door and forget about your self. My mother was right about many things, yet I sometimes wonder if she was right to say that we should forget our mirror image as quickly as we can so that we will face the world in the best womanly way possible.

Imagine with me a different scene from the mirror image you faced this morning. I'm thinking of a picture of a princess in a castle. It is a moving picture. As the princess enters the throne room on a sunny morning there is a solid bank of mirrors all along the wall to her right. As she passes by the wall of mirrors she glances at them. She doesn't mind that people see her looking in the mirror. She gazes at herself. Is she vain? Can you catch her expression? She smiles. Then, she swishes down a corridor of court admirers to attain the Presence of her father, the king.

Perhaps your life is more like mine. There are no long banks of mirrors featured on high castle walls. There is no corridor of courtly attendants celebrating the moment I enter the room, though perhaps children and grandchildren (ours and other people's) come a close second to a royal group in waiting, which is why growing older as a woman is such a blessing. If you and I look into a mirror at all, outside the privacy of bedroom and bath, a fleeting and disapproving glare may stare back from the glass. We certainly do not want to get caught looking at our selves.

Now there are all sorts of reasons why our lives are not like a princess's life. I'm sure you can think of some. I can. I have no servants waiting to breakfast and dress me for one thing. I do not have a cohort of people whose work it is to make sure I feel good about myself. If Princess Diana instructed us at all, having all that help doesn't ensure a woman will be happy in her heart.

But I want you to compose a picture of yourself. You are striding along and a solid wall of mirrors on your right hand side reflects your movements. What do you see when you catch your image in mirrors that inevitably show up in life? What is the look on your face as you gaze at your self? What is it like to have your life pass you by in the mirror? Some of our mirrors are friends, husbands, bosses, co-workers and children, as well as the picture we draw of our selves. What do these mirrors reflect? What do you see, think and feel as you look at your reflection?

Scripture says that those "who listen to the word [of God] but do not do what it says are like people who look at their faces in the mirror and, after looking at themselves, go away and immediately forget what they look like. But those who look intently into the perfect law that gives freedom, and continue to do this, not forgetting what they heard, but doing it—they will be blessed in what they do" (James 1: 23-25). We have many mirrors to choose among in our everyday lives. Which mirror will you gaze into today? How will you regard your self?

*Lord Jesus Christ, Son of God, have mercy on me, as I gaze into Your mirror today. Let me see my self as you see me.*

# 2

# MIRRORING TRUST

*John 2:23-25*

Looking at our selves is an important part of listening to God. We look in mirrors to see how to be free in Christ. We look in many mirrors, comparing our reflection, to secure the freedom that Christianity offers to us. We gaze into the perfect law of God as well as into plain mirrors in our lives, whether they are simple reflective glass or people around us. We look in mirrors to see what it means to be loved by God, and to love God. How we feel as we gaze at these mirrors affects whether or not the seeds of our love for God will grow into mature faith. As we gaze at God, we flourish in the garden of our hearts. We look in a mirror before we go out and garden in the backyard; the same is true before we garden the heart. First let's think more about mirrors.

Every morning may have a mirror in it but should we trust mirrors to reflect the truth about us? I want to focus on trust as the most intelligent response we can make to life. Gardening our hearts requires that we try out trust. What is trust? In John 2:23-25 we read: "Now while [Jesus] was in Jerusalem at the Passover Feast, many people saw the miraculous signs he was doing and believed in his name. But Jesus would not entrust himself to them, for he knew all people. He did not need human testimony about them, for he knew what was in people." Jesus was cautious not gullible. We look to him to show us how to trust other people and even how to trust our selves.

From one perspective, Jesus put trust in unusual people and doing so had amazing results as well as disastrous ones. His disciples did not know what to make of some people he trusted—like the woman at the well—the one from Samaria. Jesus revealed his identity to her. Her story is in John 4:1-42. He asked her for a drink of water and they got talking. Eventually she said: "I know that Messiah (called Christ) is coming. When he comes, he will explain everything to us. Then Jesus declared, "I who speak to you am he." This is remarkable. He met a strange woman at a well and he entrusted his identity to her, even before the twelve disciples figured out who he was. Jesus knew what he was doing and he shows us how to exercise the intelligence of trust.

But there is a warning: Christians beware. Trust is risky—even for Jesus who was human and divine. Jesus entrusted himself to his disciples—to the twelve—as well as to other people, such as Mary and Martha. Yet one of the twelve he chose himself (after praying all night) betrayed him. Judas handed Jesus over to suffering. Judas betrayed Jesus. Trust is dangerous. But without trust there is no growth toward the fullness of life in Christ Jesus. And further, trust must be learned. Mary and Martha had to learn to trust Jesus. Every Christian must eventually come to see that, although it is risky, without trust there is only hard soil in the garden of our hearts.

How are you doing with trust? Trust is fundamental in a child's life. We learned early to trust or mistrust the world, other people, and even our selves. We learned that others are safe or unsafe places to find rest. Intelligent trust requires us to understand what trust is not, as well as what it is. When we see the big picture for trust, we can sense where to locate our selves on a continuum of trust versus mistrust. I invite you to prayerfully consider your own sense of the safety or danger of trust. Our freedom to trust God is liberated or limited by what we have learned about trusting other important people in our lives.

*Lord Jesus Christ, Savior, liberate my trust in you.*

# 3

# ON ONE HAND,
# WHAT TRUST IS NOT

*James 1:5*

If Jesus was careful with trust, we should be cautious as well. To be thoughtlessly trustful does not encourage good spiritual growth in the garden of our hearts. In what follows, I will uncover differences between trust, gullibility and cynicism. Trust is a pathway between two extremes. On the one hand, it is possible to be gullible; on the other, it is possible to be cynical. Being gullible or cynical will not lead to maturity in the Christian life. Let's see what these extremes look like.

Being GULLIBLE

- is other focused
- is self-disregarding
- gives what the other person says the most weight
- believes everything
- jumps to conclusions
- shifts from one quick judgment to another without counting the cost
- is rash
- is unpredictable
- easily gives one's self away
- exercises unreflective behavior
- lives without hope
- is optimistic
- is hasty

- acts quickly
- is perpetually open
- is anxious due to worry
- accepts any evidence, however small, but does not really look for evidence
- generalized gullibility is not an asset in Christian community
- there is a time dimension in gullibility: impatient, won't wait for evidence
- refuses to count the cost in advance of taking action
- immediately accepting of other people
- attempts everything

Jesus revealed differences between trust and gullibility. He sent the disciples out and "gave them authority to drive out evil spirits and to heal every disease and sickness" (Matt 10:1). His instructions show he trusted them. In verse 5, we read that they were to choose a worthy house in each town and stay there. On entering, they gave it their greeting. Depending on the household's response, they let their peace rest on it. If their message received no welcome, they let their peace return to them, shaking the dust of that place off their feet as they left. We are not to accept mindlessly any and every reaction, as if everything was of equal value. In our culture, this instruction sounds harsh. We are relativists. We think we are supposed to accept everything as a way to be good women. If we wish to be mature, we must be *wise as serpents and as innocent as doves*. Wisdom is not gullible. Christ's trust is wise. If you think about gullibility as a hindrance to trust, what do you need to reconsider in your responses to life?

*Lord Jesus, Son of God, instruct my heart so that my trust in you, in others and in myself will grow wise.*

# 4

# ON THE OTHER HAND, WHAT TRUST IS NOT

*Genesis 4:6-7*

Trust is not gullible; neither is it cynical. Yet the very idea of trust has risk involved in it, so that trust is more like being gullible than like being cynical. If extreme gullibility stunts growth in the heart's garden because we refuse to exercise any caution, cynicism is like a killing frost that nothing survives. Our culture puts a premium value on cynicism that makes it hard to take risks if we might look foolish. Those of us who have to face daily tasks in the marketplace are driven by buyer beware signs at every turn. A worldly perspective assumes if people are really smart, they will be cynical. The worst worldly flaw is to look foolish. But Jesus took risks with his disciples. He trusted them, although he knew simple trust looks foolish to the world.

Jesus was not cynical but he did have doubts, so doubt itself is not sin. He actually wondered whether faith would survive on earth. Doubt and cynicism are not the same. Doubt is built into faith. Faith is not absolute certainty. When we are absolutely certain about something, we don't need to exercise faith. Faith asks questions and waits for an answer. God asks *us* why questions and listens to our answers. God asked Cain, "Why are you angry?" (Gen.4.6). God is not cynical. God is the author of hope. Asking a why question is very different from being cynical. So what is cynicism?

19

Being CYNICAL

- is self-focused
- is self-preserving: stubbornly refuses to give one's self to others
- refuses to give what others say any weight
- refuses to be caught out as foolish or wrong
- believes nothing
- never arrives at a final judgment
- refuses any risk
- is capricious
- lives without hope
- is pessimistic and unmoved by other people's needs
- is anxious due to anger
- believes nothing that cannot be shown
- thinks that no evidence will suffice
- treats all evidence with suspicion
- is suspicious of other people
- won't stop waiting for evidence before acting
- relentlessly skeptical
- attempts nothing

What is the condition of your heart? Is its soil hardened by cynicism? Have you tried so hard to please other people, including God, that you have turned away from trying what you have found to be pointless? Hope calls to you. Will you listen?

Are you hurt by someone who is hardened by cynicism? Let hope and trust nurture the soil of your own heart so that you have sufficient food for your own heart and some left to share with others. Cry out to God:

*Jesus, who loves me, have mercy on me.*

# 5

# WHAT IS TRUST LIKE?

*Matthew 20:29-34*

If we would be trustful we must learn to recognize extremes in our selves and prayerfully ask God to help us move to the middle, where Christ dwells, waiting for us to join him. How do you describe your self? Where do you fit on the continuum between cynical and gullible? Perhaps you have a strong tendency that you recognize right away. Perhaps you are different, depending on the situation. What is trust like?

Being TRUSTFUL

- is relational
- has a hopeful approach to life and other people
- is dialogical, conversational with others
- is willing to be wrong but aims to make a sound judgment
- is willing to revise judgments and be reciprocal
- is not hasty, but willing to act on judgments
- is willing to take risks
- is discerning
- is a non-anxious presence
- is able and willing to believe on some basis but looks for evidence
- interprets evidence effectively
- has time, is neither rushed nor lazy
- recognizes and understands how sin operates in people and social systems
- knows that the world is a beautiful and a sinful place

- continues to offer love
- takes care of essentials
- tries something

Our example of trust is Jesus. Study his responses to people in Scripture.

Consider the mother of Zebedee's sons. She knelt before Jesus to ask a favor. Was it a power play? "What is it you want?" he asked. With her sons, she came to ask whether one might sit on his right and the other on his left in his kingdom. I imagine Jesus stretching out his hand to lift her up, standing with her in solidarity, then speaking to her boys. He did not rebuke or encourage them. He said to the young men: "You don't know what you are asking." (Matt. 20.20-27). When their scheme was discovered, the other disciples were indignant. Jesus called them together and explained a higher way to all of them. Trust is tough and durable. Trust responds to what is behind a request and does not dishonor people who desperately want something. Trust understands that we are human and that being human is good. Yet trust remains focused on what is higher and better than what many of us think we want. Trust has priorities, lovingly conveyed.

If you want to learn to trust appropriately, there is no substitute for knowing Christ. What is it you want? Jesus is asking you that question. What will you say in response? Will you tell him? Will you trust him and wait for an answer? In probing the heart of what we want, self-understanding will grow.

*Lord Jesus Christ, Son of God, have mercy on me. Revitalize the soil in the garden of my heart so that I can come to trust you with everything that has life there.*

# 6

# MIRRORS MATTER

*Mark 12:41-44*

Looking in a mirror is not a simple matter. Mirrors, in a woman's life, shape her experience and the experiences of those around her. In addition, the way we act as a mirror for others, especially for the young, can encourage or discourage their capacity to know God, as they are fully known by God. If we examine some of the twentieth century influences on women, in terms of how we perceive ourselves, it is impossible to ignore Sigmund Freud. His name is known to most people. He provided an important part of the environment in which we come to name human experience. His views are like a mirror women look into; he influenced how all women see themselves.

Many researchers, his own granddaughter included,[1] say that as significant as he was, Freud was not a woman's best friend. Our disappointment with Freud has two sources: the first is the way he thought about female experience and the second is his research on how concepts of God form in children. At the heart of Freud's psychoanalytic theory is an anti-woman bias. For him, since women are not men, they are inferior. Their inferiority seeps into all aspects of life. Freud has influenced most of our thinking about our selves. But Freud is not God. God loves women as much as God loves men, not more and not less. How will you exercise your equal value in God's sight, despite living in the aftermath of a culture in which Freud's thought was so pervasive?

The second problem Freud injected into western culture is the exclusion of mothers from the formation of concepts for God. A woman's concept of God (and every human being has a concept of God, whether or not it is favorable) strongly affects her self-image and self-esteem. How we feel about our selves has a lot to do with the way we believe God looks at us. What is the expression on God's face, when God looks at you? Jesus shows us God's face. We look to Christ as our example of how God looks at us. We must ask: How shall I regard my self?

Jesus observed a woman who gave what she had, a small coin—a tiny coin of money. He knew this was her whole reserve. He praised her gift above other wealthy gifts given to the temple treasury. Jesus' gaze searched out a woman who had been hemorrhaging for many years and found her. When he encountered her directly, he affirmed the faith that moved the timidity that touched his clothing, a touch she thought would surely heal her. And it did. He conversed with another woman who wanted his help. He replied: "Why should I give it to you? I came to the Jews, and you are not a Jew." Taken out of context, his words seem shocking. What startled those around him was that Jesus talked to a woman at all. In talking with her, he allowed her to say what was on her mind. *Well, Jesus. Even the dogs under the table get the children's crumbs.* She was brilliant! Jesus was not put off by her verbal come back. He did not silence her tongue. He collaborated with her insight to secure her healing. He answered her prayer for her daughter.

What was it that gave women courage to press close to Jesus and to speak to him? I suggest it was the way he looked at them. His gaze welcomed responsive hearts so they could put hope in him. We gaze at God with Jesus in mind. What is the expression, as God gazes at you? What do you see, think and feel as you face God?

*Lord Jesus Christ, lover of my soul, have mercy on me.*

# 7

# MIRRORING HOPE

*Luke 1:39-45*

Freud ignored the foundational role that women play in helping to construct a child's concept of God. This bedrock role is best described as mirroring, in which a mother gazes at her baby and what she looks like, that is, the look on her face, is related to what she sees there—in her baby. A baby begins to see itself as it is seen. An infant's need is to be seen as beautiful, wonderful and attractive. If infants do not receive the blessing of a mother's gaze, the effects of the loss are felt deeply. But God is gracious, and even a tiny baby is not helpless.

Gaze behavior between a mother and child is called "affect attunement." The mother and the baby work out their relationship without using words. They use a form of communication that relies on making sounds and gestures, but especially relies on the eyes. Even little infants can initiate, sustain and terminate an encounter by using their eyes alone. Babies can look at their mother's face, turn their heads and look at an object in the room, so that they get their mother's attention focused on that object with them. Their eyes can glaze over until their mother realizes this little visit has come to an end. It is a beautiful sight to observe a mother gazing at her baby.

It is as if mothers can draw out of our very being what we become. Gaze behavior helps infants form the most basic beliefs they hold about themselves and the world, and also helps form their representation of God. Mirroring is the first step. In gaze behavior, when mother and infant interact, if the mother's face is unresponsive, the mirror (her face) is a thing to be looked at and not into. To create a healthy sense of who God is, and who the child is, the infant's gaze must pass through the mirror (a mother's face) to where the real mother dwells.[2] The child needs to sense there is something more than a face to look at: behind the face is a person who has an interior (a soul) to look into. This complex experience also grounds children's belief in their own personal interior. A foundational result of a positive experience with affect attunement is the formation of hope and trust in a child's heart.

To live in the world without adequate mirrors is to be cast aside, neglected; it is to be profoundly unhappy and to lose hope. Hope is the crowning attribute of a positive disposition toward God. Hope is foundational to the courage required to act on what God is calling us to do. But hope is neither optimistic nor pessimistic. Hope is wise. Optimism assumes that everything is possible and burns out trying to do *everything*. Pessimism assumes that nothing is possible and rusts out trying *nothing*. Hope is cautious enough to believe that some things are possible but knows that life is complex. Hope sets out to see what is possible and tries to succeed at *something*.

Christ is our mirror. As we gaze at ourselves in Christ, may we see that the Scripture is true: "Christ in you, the hope of Glory. Our hope in Christ is an anchor for the soul, firm and secure" (Heb 6.19). Faith itself is being sure of what we hope for and certain of what we do not see (Heb 11:1) with ordinary vision. Faith is like the eyes of an infant gazing at its mother, seeing beyond the surface to an inner reality in which God's loving gaze conveys that we too are God's beloved children.

Do you have the courage to be hopeful today? Trust is based on hope. What is *something* God is calling you to be today?

*Lord Jesus Christ, Son of a Loving Father, give me courage to hope.*

# 8

# TRUST IS BASED ON HOPE

*Luke 1:46-55*

A trustful person is a hopeful person. Being hopeful is not the same as being optimistic and is very different from being pessimistic. For the time being, I will call a person of hope, a hopist.

A hopist says to a pessimist that if something is to be done, we must give our attention to the potential in things. We cannot dismiss people or the world in general by giving up in advance.

I think of Jesus when he first met one of the young men who would become his disciple. He gave him a new name. Jesus called him Peter because he had hope in the rock he saw beneath the young man's tumultuous, impatient, erratic surface. Jesus sees the heart. He remained faithful to Peter, even when Peter denied him. Hope is faithful but not blind. Hope understands that life is complex. Jesus lost Judas. Not everything we want can be secured. A hopist says to an optimist that life is complex. There may be degrees of accomplishment in what we feel called to do. Optimists try everything. Pessimists try nothing. Hopists try something. Hope relies on trust.

Trust is confidence in or reliance on some quality or attribute of a person or thing, or the truth of a statement. Confidence refers to a firm trust. Trust is related to confidence and faith in God, on whom we feel dependent; it has a religious source. Trust is similar to faith. Both concepts rely on a vague, partial understanding of something or someone. Yet faith is not passive acceptance of the unknown; it is a strategic decision to take a risk even when we are uncertain. Faith always has non-rational and incalculable elements and carries an element of duty to keep the faith as the foundation of social life. Trust is a form of faith. Trust invests confidence in what is likely to happen, expressed through commitment, which is more than mere cognitive understanding. Trust is a way of loving the world and those in it. Trust is a way of loving our selves.

Trust is more than personal; trust is social. Social trust is a community asset. Social trust says: I'll do this for you now, without expecting anything immediately in return, perhaps without even knowing you, confident that down the road, you or someone else will return the favor. In a trusting community, other things being equal, people, communities and social systems flourish. A society or a neighborhood that relies on a fair exchange of social trust is more efficient than a distrustful society. Trust and honesty lubricate the inevitable frictions of social life. With trust, making decisions is easier. Work gets done more effectively. People who trust others are all round good citizens. A generally trustful community or neighborhood expresses fair play towards strangers.

The following expressions of trust are different but related:

- trust in those we love, including God
- trust in authorities, systems
- trust in other people
- trust in our selves

We must learn and unlearn many things before trust flourishes in our hearts. We find it easy or hard to trust, depending on our experience. Our inner wounds offer a constant reminder that hope is not blind optimism.

*Jesus, Wounded Healer, gaze with me at my wounds and give me hope.*

9

# THE CONCEPT OF TRUST

*Mark 9:17-24*

When we exercise trust, we place a degree of confidence in someone or something that we decide to count on. Trust always has an object. We put trust in a person or a thing. Therefore, trust is a relational concept. Depending on our past experience with people or things that we put trust in, our trust grows in confidence or withers into mistrust. No one goes out of their way to be mistrustful. If others let us down, we become mistrustful. If you meet someone who has a hard time placing trust in God or in other people, there is a sorrowful story behind their reluctance—and disappointment. What is your story about trust?

As an attitude, trust is not motivated by coercion or force. Our trust can be earned but we cannot be forced to trust someone. As soon as someone tries to compel us, we no longer trust them, because we sense we are being manipulated. We cannot buy someone's trust. Trust, in order to be trusting, must be freely given and freely received. As a verb, trust is the activity of placing confidence in a person or thing and has an objective in mind or a reason for exercising trust:

- I trust my mother because I know she loves me.
- I trust letter carriers to bring my mail everyday because they are dependable; that is, they bring the mail everyday. If my mail doesn't show up when it should, there is a reason.
- I trust a new colleague to engage in reciprocal, fair exchanges so we can work together.

29

The sentences above convey different aspects of trust. Without trust, life is simply not possible. Someone who is trustworthy is willing to fulfill obligations that are crucial for cooperation. Trust enables cooperation, yet cooperation is a by-product of trust as well as its source. Trust also has to do with predictability: letters carriers always come, trains are generally on time, most of the colleagues I have worked with have been cooperative. People who have not enjoyed reasonably predictable relationships find trust a major challenge.

But even for people whose experience has been good, trust involves uncertainty. Trust is future oriented. Trust is confident anticipation that something good with happen. Trust makes us wait. Waiting and trusting go together. As well, with both trust and hope, risk is inescapable. If we could control other people we would not need to trust them. If we cannot learn to be trustful, despite a degree of uncertainty, we cannot be well—not physically, spiritually or emotionally.

To be trustful is to learn to live with some uncertainty. With the man who asked Jesus to heal his son, we say: "Lord, I do believe. Help me overcome my unbelief "(Mark 9:24). When that man came for help he said: help my son, if you can. Jesus heard the uncertainty in his voice. Jesus repeated the man's words: "If you can? Everything is possible for one who believes."

How do you respond when Jesus says that everything is possible? What is in your heart? Take a compassionate look. So much depends on a response that accurately measures the condition of your heart. You do not need to pretend you have faith that you cannot muster. Tell Jesus the truth. He responds with kindness.

*Lord Jesus Christ, Maker of Heaven and Earth: secure my belief. Help me with my unbelief: In your name; for your glory—that I might live out of the trust that comes from you.*

# 10

# A TRUSTFUL HEART

*Matthew 15:10-11*

Trust is fundamental in life. We learn early to trust or mistrust the world, other people, and even our selves. We learn early that others are safe or unsafe places to find rest for our weary souls and deep secrets. When we see the big picture for trust, we can sense where to locate our selves on a continuum of trust versus mistrust. I invite you to consider prayerfully your own sense of the safety or danger of trust. Our freedom to trust God is liberated or limited by what we have learned about trusting other important people in our lives. We do not learn trust by separating our selves from the world. This is true for two reasons. The first is that trust is a relational concept—it is learned in relationship. The second reason has to do with Jesus. He urged us to live *in* the world as he did and not in isolation from it.

If you want to learn to trust mirrors, whether they hang on washroom walls or they are faces of those you love and strangers you meet, it is necessary to look within your own heart. What lives in your heart? What flourishes there? Jesus said: "Out of the overflow of the heart, the mouth speaks" (Matt 12:34). He said this to people who lived life outwardly. The Pharisees and teachers of the Law of his day were very careful about cleansing themselves, washing their hands, clothes and bodies. They did not think washing saved them. They believed they were part of God's Kingdom by birth and conversion. But purification was part of a life style that kept them separate from the world. They thought outward purity protected

31

them from sinful and contagious contact with the world.[3] Food rules protected them from contamination as well. They were careful to protect themselves. In contrast, Jesus directed attention away from outward signs of purity and food rules and focused on the heart. He said: "What goes into your mouth does not defile you, but what comes out of your mouth, that is what defiles you" (Matt 15:10). His words remain central. It is purity of the heart that we can enjoy when Jesus lives within.

Observe your own heart. Consider for a moment what you feel compelled to say. The words we say to others, to ourselves, come from the heart. Unless we attend to our hearts intentionally, we may speak unbiblically. Think for a moment of someone you dislike, someone you are in conflict with at present. What is your thinking about that person like? Maybe you see images of that person humiliated in your presence and you feel satisfied. Consider a conversation you wish to have with that person. He or she says one thing; you say another, so on the conversation goes. In the debate, you score all the points. The other person is stupid or evil or whatever you wish. You have all the control. Notice your conversation. It seems real, and is satisfying, but it is partly imaginary. When you have all the control, you invent yourself and the other—motives, words, admissions.

The only way to know another person is to let them speak for themselves. You need the other to know the other. What do you feel compelled to say and do about other people? Our words and actions come out of the overflow of our hearts. Inward purity—gardening the heart—is essential for Christians as was outward purity for the Pharisees. Salvation proceeds from the inside out, not from the outside in. Gaze in the mirror. What is in your heart?

*Lord Jesus Christ, Lover of my soul, infuse my heart with trust, for the Kingdom's sake. Help me see my self with compassion.*

# PRAYER OF THE HEART
## DEVOTIONS 11-20

# 11

# PRAYER OF THE HEART

*Matthew 25:14-30*

If we focus entirely on how well we trust God, we miss the main point of Christianity. Matthew chapter five to seven describes our importance to God. Jesus speaks with good natured humor to emphasize how unnecessary it is to fear that God will forget us: "Therefore I tell you, do not worry about your life, what you will eat or drink; or about your body, what you will wear. Is not life more important than food, and the body more important than clothes? Look at the birds of the air; they do not sow or reap or store away in barns, and yet your heavenly Father feeds them. Are you not much more valuable than they? Can any of you by worrying add a single hour to your life?" (Matt 6:25-27). The main point of the Christian life is to sense that God is with us.

The main point of Christian living is to know that we are connected to God, through Jesus, who wants to find us. We love God because he first loved us. God loves first and for ever. God trusts us. Jesus trusted his followers with his identity, his deep and true 'secret' about himself. God entrusts us with spiritual gifts and talents that are needed in the Kingdom. It is perhaps more important to respond to the trust God places in us than to focus on how much we trust God. In working out the consequences of using wisely what God entrusts to us, we come to see God in new ways. Seeing God more clearly is a way forward in working out our problems with trust.

Take for example the parable of the bags of gold, (Matt. 25:14-30), sometimes called the parable of the talents. Three servants receive money from their master just before he leaves on a journey. The first person receives ten bags of gold, the second receives two bags of gold and the third receives one bag of gold. They each are expected to be responsible with what they are given. When the master returned to take stock, he gave the same reward to the ten bag servant as to the two bag servant: they both enjoyed the master's generosity. The first two servants had doubled the amounts they were given originally and both were blessed as a consequence. The third servant buried the one bag of gold and got a very different response. The master was angry. Why? Was it about the money? No. If money mattered the first two servants would have been rewarded differently. The problem was the image of the master that drove the third servant to bury the gold rather than invest it. The third one said to the master: "I knew you were a hard man, harvesting where you have not sown and gathering where you have not scattered seed. So I was afraid and went out and hid your gold in the ground. See, here is what belongs to you." The third servant thought of the master as hard and unjust. By hiding the gift the third servant got the harsh response that he h imagined during the master's absence. How we think about God matters!

We cannot take lightly the image of God that is hidden in our hearts. What is your idea of God? Does your image of God concur with Scripture? Take this opportunity to reflect on how you imagine God. Ask for the Holy Spirit's help. God gives us gifts. You are entrusted with gold. If you invite Jesus in, you have the treasure of his trust in the garden of your heart. What will you do today simply because God trusts you?

*Lord, have mercy on me, a sinner. Enter the garden of my heart and dwell with me there. I want to be sure of your presence within me. My need for you is very great. You are greater than my need.*

*Lord, strengthen my nerve. Show me you love and trust me in some way today. Let me be useful to you. Let me see you in some new way, today.*

# PRACTICING CHRIST'S PRESENCE

*Hebrews 4:14-16*

There are three ways that people sin: in thought, in word and in action. Often we only notice sin when it finally erupts in words or in action—when it is too late. We regret what we said or did and wish we had been wiser. We long to erase our mistake and start over. We feel we have lost something precious and we grieve its loss. This is partly because when words are said or actions seen we suddenly realize others are harmed. While we find forgiveness the moment we ask God for it, and although we may apologize to people, our words and actions hurt and we cannot erase them; there is disappointment that comes as we weigh the costs incurred. Even after forgiveness, regret may leave its traces in the garden of the heart. We long to be better, to act wisely and speak well. But we get tangled in the weeds of need and desire that stick to us like burrs on cotton socks.

Prayer of the heart takes Jesus' words seriously when he said that out of the overflow of the heart the mouth speaks. Prayer of the heart is the attention we give to our thoughts to decide wisely what we want to do or say. Thinking is very powerful. In the twentieth century, Sigmund Freud directed attention to human thought life[4] in an essay on the omnipotence of thinking. It is as if psychotherapy took over a concern with inner life that the Church neglected. In Western Christianity, the practice of prayer of the heart was ignored. Modern Christianity focused on belief and action and less on inner spiritual work. Thankfully, the Eastern part of Christendom retained an emphasis that tells us how to be good gardeners of the soil that grows within the heart. From the earliest Christian tradition, believers were expected to guard their hearts from thoughts that tempt toward sin in word or deed. Guarding the heart was a first line of attack so that sin would not overwhelm the faithful. I use the expression "gardening the heart" instead of "guarding the heart," because I understand more about gardens than war, yet the central ideas are similar.

We garden the heart with the help of the Holy Spirit. We garden the heart by observing ourselves and by listening to God. In prayer of the heart, we pay attention to a conversation with God in which we listen to the way God speaks to us. I invite you to consider your own heart as the site of some of your best efforts at weeding, planting, pruning, fencing and watering. We can become attentive to our own hearts like a mother attuned to the least sound of her baby in the crib, even as she talks on the phone or vacuums the carpet.

Prayer of the heart is a practice of discipline that enables us to find the fulfillment in loving God that we long for. Prayer of the heart isn't easy but it is simple. In prayer of the heart, Christians pay attention to what goes into and comes out of their hearts and invite the Holy Spirit to help garden the good soil God put there. Our primary gardening tool is a prayer the lame man prayed as he saw Jesus coming his way: "Lord Jesus Christ, Son of God, have mercy on me." That lame man was remarkable. He was so desperate to reach Jesus, he ignored crowds around him that tried to shut him up and push him back. We have far too many voices within— mental chatter—that crowd, accuse, abuse, insult and silence our tiny, lame attempts to get to Jesus. When we learn prayer of the heart, we attend to the longing within that cries out for Jesus—we listen to it and follow its urgings.

*Lord Jesus Christ, Son of God, have mercy on me and hear my prayer.*

# 13

# THE JESUS PRAYER
# (OR THE BREATH PRAYER)

*Hebrews 9:11-14*

The Jesus Prayer is the means by which we attune our selves to what is in the heart. In saying the Jesus Prayer, we consciously invite Christ into the moment and ask for mercy. Henri Nouwen said: "Such a simple, easily repeated prayer can slowly empty out our crowded interior life and create the quiet space where we can dwell with God. It can be like a ladder we can descend into the heart and ascend to God."[5] As we climb down into that quiet conversational place with God, we weep with the sheer relief at finally being alone with God. Our tears wash our hearts clean before the Lord.

Finding that quiet place takes practice. Many voices yammer for our attention. There is a voice that says, "Prove that you are a good person." Another voice says, "You'd better be ashamed of yourself." There is also a voice that says, "Nobody really cares about you," and one that says, "Be sure to become successful, popular and powerful." But underneath all these often very noisy voices is a still, small voice that says, "You are my Beloved, my favor rests on you." That is the voice we most of all need to hear. To hear that voice, however, requires special effort; it requires solitude, silence and a strong determination to listen. That is what prayer of the heart is; it is listening to the voice that says, "You are my Beloved."[6]

We descend into that quiet, lush garden as we pray: *Lord Jesus Christ, Son of God, have mercy on me.* The word mercy in English is the translation of the Greek word *eleos*. This word has the same ultimate root as the old Greek word for oil, or more precisely, olive oil; a substance that was used extensively as a soothing agent for bruises and minor wounds. The oil was poured onto the wound and gently massaged in, thus soothing, comforting and making whole the injured part. The Hebrew word, which is also translated as *eleos* and mercy is *hesed*, and means steadfast love. The Greek words for "Lord have mercy", are *Kyrie eleison*, that is to say, Lord, soothe me, comfort me, take away my pain, show me your steadfast love. So mercy does not refer so much to justice or acquittal, the model here is not a court room but the inner rooms of a home where children are embraced and healed. Mercy refers to the infinite loving kindness of God and his compassion for his suffering children! In confidence we pray, "Lord have mercy."[7]

The purpose of prayer of the heart is to descend into your heart and to stand in the presence of God. It is not just a time of silence, of not speaking, but of listening to God who dwells in the inner temple of the soul. It is a time to stand in God's presence. Since the incarnation of Jesus Christ, our bodies have become "temples of the Holy Spirit who dwells in us" (1 Cor 6:19); it is within our own bodies that we must seek the Spirit, within our own selves. Sanctified through Baptism and the Lord's Supper, we are grafted onto the Body of Christ. God is now to be found within. He is no longer external to us. We find God within our own hearts. As Jesus said: "Let anyone who is thirsty come to me and drink. Whoever believes in me...will have streams of living water flowing from within. By this he meant the Spirit" (John 7:37-39).

*Lord Jesus Christ, enter the garden of my heart and let flow the streams of your presence and nourish me, that I might live for you. Have mercy Lord. Refresh the dry ground, in your name.*

# 14

# WHO IS AT HOME
# IN YOUR HEART?

*James 3:13-18*

My daughter and her husband have a practice that I picked up. Anyone who makes a self-deprecating comment must pay a dollar. They keep their stash of dollars in a jar and use it to celebrate something when it accumulates. I started using the practice myself and now with my students (although I have yet to collect). Once you begin to hear how many times people abuse themselves, you will be astonished. Yet silent self-abuse is carried on in the heart, to our great collective pain, in the form of mental chatter. If God is for us who can be against us? Not even ourselves! We must include our own self-talk in the prescription to love others as Christ loves.

What do we find as we enter the sanctuary of our hearts' garden? I recall the time I discovered differences between Christian meditation and methods associated with Eastern religions. In Eastern practices there is an assumption that when one enters the heart, one is going into silence. No one else is home. You enter into the emptiness of your own experience and keep still and quiet and thereby silence the mental chatter—voices that do harm by incessant self-criticism. In contrast, Christian practices assume you are not alone in the garden of the heart; God is there with you as your partner in conversation. At first, I was distressed. As I went into the garden of my heart for solitude with God, it was as if the mental chatter turned up its volume. As we go into silence we focus our attention on what is within and we may hear voices that make us uncomfortable. How do we decide whether or not it is God speaking to us?

Often we try to decide whether the inner voices (impressions on the mind that we 'hear') are from God. This confusion can result in emotional turmoil if not trauma. When I first started to ask these questions, I remember very clearly the time, place and the event. I was in the car and my husband was driving into the city from our home in the country. I intentionally had been trying to know God more fully, even as I am fully known. But my mind was crowded with thoughts that day, such as: *Why would God love you? You are not worth what you think you are? Don't you know that you are all on your own here? No one is going to help you!* I was entirely distressed by these thoughts. Then it suddenly occurred to me that God would not speak to me in a way that was inconsistent with Scripture. Those accusations are not to be found in the Bible. They were from the Accuser, not God who is the lover of my soul. I now use two fundamental rules that help very much. The first is that God never says insulting things to me. The second is that God never tries to make me feel all alone and helpless. James tells us just the reverse: "*Submit yourselves, then, to God. Resist the devil, and he will flee from you. Come near to God and he will come near to you*" (James 4:7, 8a).

When we enter into the sanctuary of the heart's garden it is essential to notice how we speak to and about our selves. We do not go to silence but to conversation so abusive talk must be weeded out. Self-abuse is deadly. One way to de-stabilize the habit of harmful self-talk is to show our selves the compassion and grace of Christ and to trust that we are valuable to God.

*Lord Jesus Christ, have mercy. Heal the wounds of self-abuse that hinder my heart's growth. Please show me the difference between suffering in the world, for your sake, and suffering at my own hands, needlessly, because I let my inner dialogue insult me. Lord have mercy on me, your beloved one.*

# 15

# SOCIAL ABUSE CAN BECOME SELF-ABUSE

*John 8:2-11*

I went walking with a young woman the other day. We spend time together as an older woman (yes, that's me) and a younger woman, to see what we can learn together as spiritual friends. At one point she told me about recent observations of her workplace. She gave special attention in several business meetings to the different way her senior boss treated men and women. She noted that whenever men spoke, her boss waited for the man to finish and affirmed his statement in some way. Whenever women spoke, even though they were also part of senior management, her boss interrupted them. When finished, if they were allowed to finish, he repeated what they said in his own words without attributing credit to the woman. She was upset by what she saw. What are we to make of this young woman's observation? What does it say about prayer of the heart?

We know about self-abuse that hides in the heart, making it feel unsafe to engage with our own thoughts. I suggest that women also suffer social abuse that invades the gardens of our hearts and makes it hard to hear God speaking, as God longs to speak to us. Before we look at social disdain, let us hear an insight from another young woman. Both of these women are in their twenties and are confused about their place in the social world. When they were young they thought that "Women's Lib," if it was ever needed, was no longer necessary.

The second young woman wrote:

As a woman and a Christian, there have been times in my own life when I have felt disempowered on account of the gap between the personal and the social realities I face. I sometimes experience the socio-cultural world of my church as androcentric and do not always feel like I "fit" as a result. For example, it seems to me that the popular interpretation of sin as pride, wanting to be like God, self-righteousness, does not apply equally to women as to men. I experience myself differently. My failure and separation from God come about in the form of self-denial (food, sleep), lack of self-confidence, insufficient self-esteem, etc. I experience sin as an undervaluing of myself more than as an attempt to be like God. An androcentric definition of sin can disempower women by contributing to their failure or inability to identify and combat sin in their own lives. For example, I think that many Christian women are uncomfortable with and feel guilty about their own sexuality in large part because a male preoccupation with—and fear of—the sex act has meant that "sexual sin" is always at or near the top of a hierarchy of sins in most churches.[8]

The troubles that linger in the hearts of these two women are not a result of personal disrespect; they result from social disdain in a world that treats women differently from men. This is such a hard topic to face. None of us want to be seen as "those angry women" but we need to sense when we are treated disrespectfully simply because we are women. If we hope to love our selves as Christ does—if we long to love the world in Jesus' name, we see disrespect from others as a noxious weed in the garden of our hearts. It must be pulled out.

*Lord Jesus Christ, Savior, you who welcomed women, help me face my self and see your love. Turn anger that you find in my heart into insight so I may help to open up the world for other women and for any person who longs to know you face to face. I need to know that you love me as I am. Help my unbelief.*

# 16

# THE HEART OF SOCIAL DISDAIN

*John 20:10-17*

It is true that our hearts are personal property but they are formed in social contexts. We are shaped by the perceptions others have of us. I am not saying we are determined by other people's perceptions, and have no freedom, but the social world speaks loudly to us as our personal worlds are being formed. If we ask how we should regard our selves from a personal perspective, we desperately need also to ask how the world regards us, if we hope to follow Christ. In a world wallpapered with women's thin, nearly naked bodies, we are compelled to ask our selves about the effect that such as world has within the garden of a woman's heart.

When I think of social disdain I think of Mary. Scripture identified her as one out of whom Jesus cast several demons. What sort of woman is filled with demons? I don't imagine that, even after she was healed, she enjoyed social ease. Yet she loved Jesus with her whole heart. She is the one who lingered in the garden after the disciples discovered that Jesus' body was missing, three days after his crucifixion. They left. She waited. Perhaps she didn't know what else to do.

She knew she had been saved. For her, there was a very definite before and after meeting Jesus. While waiting in that garden, she heard a man she thought was the gardener. Through her tears she asked for Jesus' body. The Gardener was Jesus. And he did not say: "Oh, it's you. Well, say Mary do you know where the guys are. I

45

have something important to tell them." He said her name in a way that let her recognize him and he gave her the powerful truth of his resurrection, knowledge she could take to the others. He treated her as a credible witness—an astonishingly counter-cultural act for his context. The disciples did not treat her as a credible witness, however, and it is not entirely clear she treated herself with the same respect that Jesus did.

The social world infests the garden of the heart. The world is too much with us for us to ignore its effects. So what is to be done? In my own roller coaster history regarding the issue of social recognition, I continue to rely on reading Scripture as a way to situate my feelings and responses. I try to see Jesus' responses as a way to inform my own reaction. I have learned that feeling angry about injustice is not the same as acting in hostility due to that injustice. Feeling angry is understandable; acting in a hostile fashion is also understandable but seldom helpful to the whole community. And I want to mature in the faith. I have learned that forgiving others is significant for the well-being of Christian community. I have been saved; I am free to forgive others.

But being saved is one thing; learning to live as a saved person is another. Our initial liberation in Christ (being saved from sin) must be followed by learning how to live with that freedom day by day. Mary had to go back to town. She had to tell the disciples that Jesus rose from the dead and live through their mistrust that she was a worthy witness. She had to go on trusting that Jesus knew what he was doing when he gave her the words of life. She had to grasp the hope that Jesus knew what he was doing when he saved her in the first place. She had to hold on to her faith in Christ. She had to trust the value Jesus placed on her and in her.

*Lord Jesus Christ, lover of my soul, let me sense that you know me well enough to lead me day by day. Let me see my self as you see me. Let me know that I am not alone in the garden of my heat, that You are there.*

46

# 17

# RECOVERING YOUR HEART

*Mark 4:1-20*

I had the privilege recently to talk to two women. One is perhaps in her seventies and the other is in her twenties. Both are prodigal daughters: women who were in the Church as children but for a variety of reasons, set out on their own. Now, because God is able to speak to our hearts no matter where we are or what we are doing, they expressed a desire to come back home. They told beautiful stories of God's capacity to keep in touch with them, even while they were far away. But both of them, in different ways, expressed hesitation about coming back into Christian community, even though God was very real to them. They were afraid of other Christians. They were afraid of trying to be Christian and failing at it. They were sure about God; they weren't sure about "being Christian." What if they got hurt or disappointed? What if they couldn't do it?

I have only one response to these worries at this point in my life. It is to talk about the struggles in my own heart that I have with sin. I asked Jesus into my heart when I was twelve years old, beside my mother, kneeling at her bed. Jesus came and remains. But I continue to sin in ways that inform me about my own history, my fears, my needs and my desires. All I can do is garden my own heart and weed out thoughts that trouble the quiet of that holy place. With me, what these two wonderful women can learn to do is to garden their own hearts. All of us must try, with the Holy Spirit's help, to engage in the spring, summer, fall and winter work of heart gardening. I constantly bring to mind Jesus' words: out of the overflow of the heart the mouth speaks. I continually ask my self what I am doing at any given moment and why I feel compelled to say or do what I am considering in the seclusion of my own heart. *Lord, have mercy.*

In gardening the heart, self-knowledge is central. Frequently, when people came to him, Jesus said: What do you want me to do? That is the question. What do you want Jesus to do for you? What do you want? It is more important to know your self than it is to critique other people. When you die and stand before God you will not be asked how someone else lived his or her life. You and I are only responsible for our own reactions and responses. We are free to connect with God and to remain connected because God is willing and graciously able to give us what we need for a faithful life. James says: "If any of you lacks wisdom, you should ask God, who gives generously to all without finding fault, and it will be given to you" (James 1:5). The wisdom we need is self-understanding based on self-knowledge. Why do you sin in the ways that you do? What are you looking for? What do you lack? *Lord Jesus Christ, Son of God, have mercy on me.*

What is growing in your heart? Can you sense its beauty? What flourishes there? Where are the pleasant, green places bordered by the growth of the good seeds God planted? Jesus told parable of the sower in Mark 4:1-20. In this story a farmer sows seed that falls in various places, some on hard ground, some among weeds, some in rich soil. The parable tells us about the heart. There are many reasons why the two women I spoke with have hard soil in the gardens of their hearts. But they also have good soil. There are places in the depths of their being where God's good seed has taken root and sprouted. They must find Christian community in order for their inner work to be thoroughly nourished and blossom as a godly place.

*Lord Jesus Christ, have mercy. Show me how to be with other people that long to love you with all their hearts, just as I do.*

# 18

# FOCUSING ON BEAUTY

*Genesis 1:27-31*

The purpose of a garden is to concentrate beauty. In its loveliness, a garden offers peace and rest. Inner beauty is the gift that Christianity gives to those who love God more than any other love. When there is beauty within, we are free to enjoy beauty in the world. If hearts are crowded with weeds, if dry, hard, unfertilized soil is dominant, we are driven by an insatiable desire to work on externals, on appearing beautiful, but feeling ugly. Women are hard pressed to love themselves in a culture that is confusing for them. In particular, and as Mary Pipher points out, we live in a society that is harmful to girls.[9]

Prayer of the heart makes inner beauty possible. To focus on inner beauty is to resist the worst aspects of the culture in which we live; it is also to find the aesthetic satisfaction with our selves that many of us want. Beauty is a perennial issue for women. The opposite of beauty in Christian life is not ugliness, it is slavery. A beautiful life is not enslaved. There are two ways in which believers become enslaved. The first is by giving themselves over to other people who have plans for them that they do not have for themselves. Slavery is living life through someone else's agenda and never finding one's own way. Many people live to appease others and think they are pleasing God by doing so. To please God is to listen to God's whisper in our own hearts and to obey God, not other people. God said: "You shall have no other gods before me" (Exod 20:3).

The second way to be enslaved is by refusing to master our selves. Recall Cain: God said that sin was crouching at his door and he must master it. God expects us to master our selves with the Holy Spirit's help. A most destructive feeling we can have is to fear that our thoughts, words or actions are out of control. Discipline in the Christian life is not optional any more than an empty lot where people throw whatever they happen to have in their hands at any given moment can be called a garden. The difference between a litter strewn space and a well-tended garden is beauty.

God is love. God is the source of all that is beautiful in the world. Love is beauty. Beauty is love. Dostoyevsky wrote: "Such beauty... will ultimately save the world."[10] If there is any beauty in the world, it is a reflection of the love we see in Jesus. External beauty is a by-product of internal beauty. The fruit of the heart's produce is beauty and discipline, compassion and purpose. Believers cultivate a beautiful soul, with God's help. Augustine of Hippo wrote, "The beauty of everything is in a way their voice by which they praise God."[11] When God created the world, with you in mind, God saw everything and it was very good; the word for good in Greek means beautiful.[12]

What is the source of beauty in your life? Where can you find it? Where are you looking? If you are caught up in the fear of your own face, you can find relief by tending the garden of your own heart. The Lord is near. God knows you and loves you. There is no shame in your life that God cannot make beautiful. Of this, I am confident.

*Lord Jesus Christ, Savior, let me look at my self and see you in my own countenance. Let me know you are here with me, for sure. Fill my heart with the beauty of your Presence and Grace. Let me cultivate your divine love, for the Kingdom's sake, and for my own sake. Garden my heart with me. Till this dry, litter strewn soil. Refresh me.*

# 19

# HARDY GARDENS AND NOXIOUS WEEDS

*2 Peter 1:3-8*

C an you recognize noxious weeds in your heart's garden? The heart unites thinking, willing, feeling and doing. In tending the heart, we focus on thinking. We are tempted to allow thought to be used against our will? First, the enemy reminds us of people who have wronged or offended us. He tries to present all the insults, wrongs and injuries inflicted on us in brilliant color. He points out the necessity for retaliation and resistance; he says: demand justice, common sense, the public good, self-preservation and self-defense. The enemy tries to shake the very foundation of prayer, namely forgiveness and meekness (disciplined strength) so that weeds will crowd out the good growth in our hearts. A person who is full of resentment and does not forgive her neighbor is hindered from obtaining forgiveness when she prays—not that forgiveness is ever unavailable, but it is harder to access under these conditions. The one who tries to pray under these conditions can't even concentrate on prayer. Angry thoughts dissipate prayer. The seeds of God's word are blown away. Good growth in the heart cannot flourish.[13] If we seek beauty, we must confront sin. Sin produces slavery. The Eastern medieval Church understood sin and analyzed it fully, and here is the process.

The mind receives a thought which is a suggestion or stimulation. If the mind is attentive, it will notice the provocation (temptation) and will close the door on it. If not, then, the soul will dialogue with the suggestion and give assent to it (as Eve did with the Serpent and as Adam did with Eve's offer), whereupon it becomes sinful because it consents to the thought with some pleasure.

At this point, there is union or coupling with the thought in which the mind surrenders itself to the suggestion and begins to dwell upon it. The mind is made captive by the thought as it readily consents to it time and again.

Finally we fall so completely under the power of the suggestion that we are no longer free to resist it. It becomes a passion. We become its slaves. [14]

When we allow the gardens of our hearts to be overgrown with noxious weeds, we cannot focus on anything but their pervasive presence. We fix our gaze on them, and as much as we detest them, they take our full attention. We are so fascinated by a weedy garden within that we lose touch with the world in which we can act courageously to secure justice, mercy and peace for others and for our selves, all for the Kingdom's sake. But the good news is that the gardens of our hearts can be weeded daily and moment by moment, so that the good seeds can grow and flourish. Then, we are free to be as God intended.

Be free to be what you are! By grace, you are God's beloved. Act out of that love. You have Life implanted in you. Express it! His love is spread abroad in your heart. Show it in what you think, do and say! Grace has made you graceful. Let every word and act express that beauty. "You are washed, you are anointed, you are sanctified.... Be what you are! Work out your salvation with fear and trembling. For it is God who is at work within you, both to will and to do that which is pleasing to Him."[15] Gardening the heart, with God's help, leaves its impression on the face.

*Lord, let your beauty shine on my face that others might see you and want to know who You are.*

# 20

# GARDENING WITH GOD

*1 John 4:7-12*

God surprises us with love. It is odd that the creator of the universe would come to dwell in your heart, and my heart, but that is the Christian message.

> "For God so loved the world that he sent his one and only Son, that whoever believes in him shall not perish but have eternal life. For God did not send his Son into the world to condemn the world, but to save the world through him. Whoever believes in him is not condemned...those who live by the truth come into the light, so that it may be seen plainly what they have done has been done in the sight of God" (John 3:16-18, 21).

It is hard to garden in the dark. Let the light of Christ's love shine on your heart so that you can see what you are doing.

Gardening the heart is the work we do to see to it that our thought life is holy, pure and beautiful. Jesus turns our attention away from other people and focuses with us on our thoughts, words and actions. The faithful pay more attention to their own hearts than they do to the failure and harm that other people commit. It is not that we develop laissez-faire attitudes about what other people do; rather we aim to enlist God's help in keeping our own gardens clear of noxious weeds. If we begin with our own hearts we are better able to sense what can be done in the world, for God's sake.

What are the weeds that grow in your garden? They are words, gestures, glances, expressions, postures, silences, strategies and overt actions (your own, as well as other people's) that rob us of the quiet pleasure of being fully present to God. Prayer of the heart digs around in the hard soil of our hearts and gets a grip on weeds and with the help of God's Holy Spirit, pulls them out. It is possible to pull out the weeds that like to grow in your heart. They come out with effort—and effortlessly because of God's almighty power—quickly or eventually, stem, root and all.

Even if our ordinary experience is relatively peaceful and happy, weed seeds float over the garden of our hearts, blown by the winds of culture and circumstance, and settle into soft good soil that we cultivated for other purposes. Sin, as the circulating harm that infests the world, has a way of finding a place in the heart, regardless of a gardener's skill and attention. But weeds do not have to sprout and grow; even if they grow for a short time (with amazing speed) they do not have to remain. Pull them out. You can do this. With God's help, you can garden your own heart.

If you love God, remember that you are in the business of cultivating a beautiful inner garden, with God's help. Never be so focused on what makes life difficult, that you become preoccupied with what you think cannot be done. Never be so dazzled by ideals that you talk your self into lying about the way things are. Keep ever before you the thought that you are beloved by God.

*Lord Jesus Christ, help me focus not on how I feel about my self but on how much I love you. Loosen the grip that fear has on me. Let me know that your love for me endures all things, believes all things, hopes all things and will bring me into your Presence to enjoy you, now and forever. My need for you is very great. And you are greater than my need. Lord, have mercy on me and show me how to love you with all my heart, in your name and for your sake, Amen.*

54

# WHAT DOES GOD REQUIRE?

## A SHORT STORY

# WHAT DOES GOD REQUIRE?

Once there was a woman who was spiritual. People knew that and came to her for prayer. It was her habit to spend time with God one day each month in silent retreat. She went to a retreat house she used so often she thought of it as her own. Her room had a private bathroom and comfortable furniture.

One month she decided to work on what Scripture says about love. The next retreat day, love was still the subject. She scanned her notes and arranged the furniture in the room, adjusting things, just so. She sat down in her favorite chair to pray. Oh, the mirror! Her chair was across the room from a dresser with a large mirror attached to the back of it. She couldn't pray if she saw her own image in the glass. She got up and tilted the mirror so she couldn't see her self. The day passed in quiet reflection, reading, meditating, walking outside on well-tended grounds, praying a favorite prayer: Lord Jesus Christ, Son of God, have mercy on me.

In the afternoon, a strange thing happened. She was sitting in her chair again and the Lord spoke: *"I want you to wash your face."* What? She laughed. Wash my face? You're not serious. She shook her head free of the voice. *"Wash your face."* What are you saying? You're not serious. Is this You? What are you asking? Some moments passed. God was near. She listened. *"Wash your face."*

My face? I can't do that. People will see me. If anyone looked at me washed, they would see what I'm really like. I can't take off the cover I so carefully put in place. You don't know what you're asking.

She waited listening, wanting to be let off. The silence was full of Presence. Just wash, you say. It is not that simple. I'll have to meet people like that, without covering my face...No! But she washed her face. She ran her fingers over smooth skin on her cheeks. Why was that so hard? The day was nearly over and there were so few words written in her notebook. Her face was clean. She wasn't sure what that act meant but responding to God was always such a relief.

She tidied the room, about to leave, yet something still needed to be done. She couldn't put her finger on it. She sat down in her chair and looked up. She forgot to put the mirror back in place. She adjusted it and sat down. She could see her own face. A clean face, like many others, but she knew it well. *"Pray for that face."* What? What are you asking? What would I say? *"How do you pray for others?"* I pray by listening to You, by lifting another person up to You. *"With eyes wide open to My mercies, pray for this face."* She gazed at her face. Lord Jesus Christ, come and visit your servant. She supplied her own name as she prayed for that clean, uncovered face.

Friends, who is this God we worship? We serve a God who invites us to offer compassion to our selves in the same way we are asked to love others. Can you do this? Will you try?

Every morning has a mirror in it. That mirror in our hearts is Jesus. What do you see when you look at your reflection in that Mirror? You can trust that Mirror. It is entirely possible to see the love of Christ, for you, shining back as you gaze at your face in any mirror that you wish to look in. May this be true for you, in the quiet of your own heart.

*Even so, come Lord Jesus.*

# EVERY DAY HAS A DOOR HANDLE IN IT

## DEVOTIONS 21-30

# 21

# EVERY DAY HAS A DOOR-HANDLE IN IT

*Matthew 4:18-22*

If you look in a mirror each morning, you also turn a door-handle each day. I suppose we can avoid mirrors if we stay in bed, but even the bathroom has a door-handle on it and entering that room is inevitable no matter how overwhelmed we feel about life in general. Most mornings we turn a door-handle and walk out into a larger world. Turning the handle of a door requires us to take action. The door-handles in our days represent decisions we make. We decide to act with intentional energy or with reluctant resignation. Either way, the door opens and we walk out into a wide world with sidewalks or dirt roads, a world packed with urban streets lined by high-rise buildings, or by neat houses in rows with alleys behind, or we walk out into the countryside that is an open reach of land, extending to the horizon—to the limits of seeing.

Each day, we turn door-handles and walk out into the world with a purpose of some kind: to work, play, shop, visit. The decisions we make act back on us and create the life we are choosing to live. Maybe we drift around shopping malls, looking for ways to spend money. Maybe we turn a door-handle and enter our own backyards to dig the dirt and plant flowers and vegetables that flourish under our care and nourish us aesthetically and physically.

What is it that drives us to turn the door-handles in a day? What is the inner strength that keeps us deciding and moving, shopping, gardening, buying, selling and setting things right? What moves us to act? Usually it is some concept we have for what makes life good plus a sense of necessity. What do you think makes life good? Are your days characterized by the dreams you had for the way you wanted life to turn out? What moves us from desire to action? What gets us from feeling and hoping to take action congruent with the best ideas we have for our selves and those we love?

There is evidence that North Americans are experiencing a widespread sense of personal powerlessness—a sort of gilded depression—a sense that life is disappointing and does not measure up to our dreams. Often this sadness takes the form of not being able to turn a door-handle to the out-of-doors world that each day offers. We seem to lie around a lot. We seem to long for a time when we can get some rest. Is that true of you? If the gardens of our hearts are weeded daily, we find it easier to turn the door-handles that lie before us and take action that needs to be done. Being busy is different from taking action in the sense that I want to explore. Being busy is not a cure for feeling disappointed with life.

Seeing the action that needs to be taken comes from a well-tended heart. In a heart full of the weeds of worry, anger, resentment and fear, it is hard to see the courageous action that needs to be taken, action that must be well-considered and wise. Is the malaise of disappointment a result of our refusal to take courageous action? Sometimes the right action is to resist abuse, whether at home or at work. Sometimes right action maintains a true and godly purpose in life rather than being sidetracked by secondary interests. Right action is revealed through a life devoted to God in communion with other believers. Right action takes courage.

*Lord Jesus Christ, gently show me what needs to be done. Inspire my heart. Let me see clearly what you are leading me to do.*

# 22

# WHY DO WE SUFFER?

*John 6:25-29*

I don't know why we are suffering from an inability to act that allows the television industry (with inexpressible ease) to keep so many of us on our couches for hours and hours each day, but I do know that we have become a society of watchers, rather than doers. This shift is a serious handicap for the Kingdom of God. I don't believe that there will be sofas in heaven. There may be couches in heaven for some people but they won't be there for those of us who have had so much comfort here on earth. And I know there won't be any television sets. We will have each other to get to know and we will see how good it is to spend time with those we love.

If you are not spending boundless time on the couch, perhaps you know someone who is—someone you live with or love. If you do spend a lot of time on the couch, please understand that you are among an increasingly large number of people. It seems to be a social phenomenon. You are not alone. You are not strange. But the question is, are you lonely?

Have Christians taken up inaction because we are afraid to make mistakes? Are we paralyzed because we have been injured, physically, emotionally or morally? Are we sedentary because we no longer encourage each other socially, extending hospitality to friends and to strangers?

I suggest that our inaction may also be due to the malaise of circulating mistrust. North America is in decline with respect to social capital (social trust). Circulating mistrust eventually turns back on the people that express it. Mistrust is a disaster for the Church.

Other current research reveals tendencies among young girls to engage in relational aggression during which they inflict emotional wounds on other people. Perhaps you saw the *New Yorker* magazine article titled, "Girls Just Want to Be Mean." Relational aggression paralyzes people, keeping them from achieving the good goals they dream about. Sometimes, the victims of female relational aggression kill themselves.[16] It would be strange indeed if we became inactive in order to prevent harm, to keep ourselves from making mistakes, and in the absence of acting, we made the world much more dangerous than it was when we were trying our best but sometimes failing, sometimes saying the wrong words, or locking the door to a prodigal child the very night she is abducted and never seen again. Understandably, we are desperately afraid of making mistakes.

As a society we abhor making mistakes. A young woman recently told me, when I asked if she resented anything about God, that (after much reflection because she did not want to admit she resented God) she realized she resented God for not making it possible for her to be perfect. She was angry at God because perfection (her ever-present life-goal) would always evade her. When she realized her resentment, she laughed at her self. Laughing at our selves is very healthy. Crying due to our human mistakes and laughing at our human limitations are both part of living within the territory of God's grace. I am certain that suffering has an indelible contribution to make to our hearts—suffering we take on willingly because we choose to and suffering that is thrust upon us because all humanity is frail, weak, broken and sinful—especially me and you.

*Lord Jesus Christ, Son of God, have mercy. Show me that your love is greater than my mistakes.*

# 23

# LOSS AND RECOVERY

*Luke 7:11-17*

We feel compelled to ask questions about suffering when circumstances are out of control. Loss is maddening and can drive us mad. We suffer from not knowing why something we counted on has failed, or something we hoped for has not arrived. Loss leaves us feeling alone and unsafe. To enjoy intimacy with God is to feel vulnerable yet safe in the arms of a Loving Father. How may we move from loneliness to safety? Like prodigal children, we come to our senses and return home so we can recover what was lost, even when losses are due to our own foolishness.

In gardening the heart we are concerned with paying attention to what is beautiful and allowing our thoughts to focus on that beauty. We also are concerned with weeding and pruning thoughts that do not contribute to the garden's loveliness. But why are there so many thoughts to distract us from God's holiness, mercy, compassion and grace? Why is sin we ruminate on so plentiful— like the prolific corner store that sells cheap candy we don't really want to consume?

Genesis provides a perspective on perennial sin. Paradise was lost, the original garden, but relationship with God was recovered— with a difference. The world has weeds. When people decided to disobey, to the woman God said: "I will greatly increase your pains in childbearing; with pain you will give birth to children. Your desire will be for your husband, and he will rule over you." To Adam God said: "Cursed is the ground because of you; through painful toil you will eat of it all the days of your life. It will produce thorns and thistles for you, and you will eat the plants of the field. By the sweat of your brow you will eat your food until you return to the ground, since from it you were taken; for dust you are and to dust you will return" (Gen 3:16-19). How do we apply that curse to our experience as modern and post-modern women?

In the West, sins that so easily entangle do not grow in ground many of us till for food; they flourish in a heart we must garden for God's sake. After humanity lost Eden, intimacy with God, our freedom and intimacy with others was also tainted. Pain and suffering is experienced in our relationships. Even with the saved, freedom is not automatic. In our "free" society "there will always be a struggle between higher and lower forms of freedom" and "the struggle goes on,"[17] this side of heaven. Engaging the struggle is a sign of hope. Taking action can change hearts and minds. Through acting courageously we can regain intimacy in Christian community. After Eden, struggle is inevitable but does not automatically defeat us. We can act.

Because of Eden we long to have intimacy with God. Due to thoughts that trouble and distress us, spiritual intimacy is hindered in its growth. What is to be done? Whenever there is loss, God replies with a promise. Jesus is the fulfillment of that promise. Christ in you the hope of Glory! In Jesus we see how to be human and we come fully to appreciate the beauty of God in our own being. Have you allowed Jesus the Christ to enter fully into that inner space in your heart where you are most completely your self? If the answer is yes, then you have only to pay attention to his presence in order to learn from him.

*Lord Jesus Christ, by the power of your word and your resurrected life, I turn my attention to you, to your words and to your example, that I might know you as I am fully known by you. Let me know the safety of being with you, now and ever more.*

# 24

# WHAT ARE WOMEN FOR?

*Proverbs 31:10-31*

If we ask what the purpose of a woman's life consists in, we might answer the question in two ways: What are women used for? What do women stand for? There is nothing more important in the Christian life than to be used by God to secure Kingdom goals. 'Being used' is ambiguous. In the twentieth century, women came to be seen as useful in a sexual sense that is hard for many to connect with spiritual intimacy, let alone with our dreams for sexual intimacy. What is going on?

In order to get a sense of what is happening at present (so we can decide what we stand for) we look back to periods of historical social change. Around the year 1100, the image of the ideal woman was changing. Prior to this, an ideal woman was a capable wife and mother who could run a household and protect an estate in the absence of her husband. This woman was not unlike the image of an ideal woman in Proverbs 31: 10-31, who is intelligent, noble, industrious, well-regarded communally and highly praised by her family. She was a shelter from the storms of life for husband and children. Her very body was an abode, a place of peace and safety. She enjoyed her giftedness and acted independently. At her breast, those she loved found satisfaction.

The change that took place in the 1100s shifted focus from an ideal of competence and safety to a heroine who was young and beautiful. Age and appearance became issues. Women's clothing changed so that a full loose covering of the body was replaced by dresses with tightly fitting bodices to reveal the female figure. Hair was cut short and small caps replaced the full head-dress of the previous period. The new style expressed an admiration for youth and beauty and was essentially a new ideal.[18] With the emergence of a new ideal, the value placed on women's lives was altered. Social changes of this type affect our understanding of what women are for.

What is happening to us right now and how do these changes affect our devotion to God? If we look at the proliferation of images of women that we cannot avoid seeing, what do we find? We see young, perfectly proportioned, extremely lean women who are most often alone. The ideal woman is always sexual—at all times, in all places, regardless of what else she is doing. Youth and beauty are celebrated, in contrast to the ideal woman of the twentieth-century war era who was much like the image in Proverbs. The shift from housewife to whore is startling and the extreme sexuality of the ideal woman is new, brought to you by the invention of contraception.

But we do not despair! We are not overwhelmed by the media women that haunt our struggle to love our own bodies as gifts from God. God does not turn away even when we go a-whoring. God remembered Israel when she whored after other gods. Jesus talked to prostitutes. There is no place that sexuality can take us where we cannot be found by our loving heavenly Father, by our friend and brother Jesus. But God did not make us for sex alone. Like our relation to bread, we do not live by sex alone but by every word that comes from the mouth of God. We need God's love more than sex. Sex cannot save us, even though the end of the twentieth century is marked by its core belief in salvation by sexuality. We find life in Christ in that strange territory between being fully human and loving the divine. We bring our own, real, messy sexuality to God and offer praise.

*Lord Jesus Christ, lover of my soul, help me not hide from you. I love you Lord.*

# 25

# MISSING DAUGHTERS

*Mark 10:13-16*

I was directing a conference recently. The schedule included a healing service. I was blessed by hearing many stories of loss and recovery, stories that conveyed the longing to restore what was or still is lost. But I was surprised by the number of women who had daughters that were missing. Either these young women had left home months ago and were still away, or they were planning to leave home, or they had just returned. What is happening to our girls? How is society making home an impossible place for women to find happiness? The influences are societal not personal. We are witnessing a trend, not a reaction to a few inadequate parents. Inadequate parenting is an issue in some families, but those who are losing their daughters to anorexia or the street or other people's houses where rules are non-existent are 'good enough' families, given the historical development of an institution that has enormous demands placed upon it now.

A good enough mother is one who actively adapts to an infant's needs, an active adaptation that gradually lessens, according to the infant's ability to account for its own failure to adapt to the environment and to tolerate the results of frustration in trying to learn from the environment.[19] Good-enough parenting begins with an almost complete adaptation which gradually lessens until parents see that the young can deal with their failure and are learning how to be themselves. We adapt to our children until they begin to grow up. Then we send them out into the world. What goes wrong often happens outside the home. When women leave home what do they find? The ideal woman at the end of the twentieth century looked more like a street girl than a home body.

What then do woman stand for? What are we called to do and to be in a world that has lost touch with what it means to be female? What does it mean to be a woman—a good enough woman?

Again we must ask what is in our hearts. What are the resentments, losses, disappointments and failures that frighten us to death and keep us from loving our children and letting them go into a world they can manage with reasonable success. We do not live our children's lives for them. But it is hard to be happy our selves when our children are in pain. Not all of us have children, but we are all affected by quality of their lives. If the young are unwell everyone pays the price.

Jesus prized children. He said that unless we become like little children we cannot enter the kingdom of God (Mark 10:15). Do we value children? Have we relegated the care of children to a lesser social role? Do you love children? Do you resent children for their demands on you? Are you afraid that all your gains as a woman will be lost if you associate with children and use your gifts there? Is it as a friend suggested: Adults are so busy being childish them selves, they have no resources left to look after the young. Children are helpless. They need our help. What is our response? What is in your heart? Out of the overflow of the heart the mouth speaks...and the body acts.

*Lord Jesus Christ, Son of God, child of a heavenly Father, one who was called beloved by your Father, let me see how I can parent in the world you have given me to love. Allow me the confidence to know that if I follow you into the world you will not let me be lost because I use my gifts for those who have little social value. Let me remember my childlike need for you. Help me listen to my own heart, not be driven by guilt, but moved by compassion.*

# 26

# THE LOST SON

*Luke 15:1-7*

I want to explore the idea that maybe we don't act courageously because we fear making mistakes. I wonder if the social pressure to "be our selves" leaves us anxiously wanting to make the perfect decision about our lives so that we take the fullest advantage of being authentic and alive to all our potential. A story in Scripture addresses the fear of making mistakes and situates the solution to human folly in a relentlessly patient Father who waits for our return.

The Lost Son story is told in a particular context. The Pharisees and teachers of the law were observing Jesus closely. They complained that he spent time with sinners and tax collectors. Why would a teacher with Jesus' authority spend time with people who were unclean, who might spoil his reputation? What was he doing? Jesus' behavior made no sense to teachers of the law. In response to their whispering, he told three stories about loss: a lost sheep, a lost coin and a lost son. In all three stories, the effort expended to find what was lost was heroic. The shepherd, the woman and the father in these stories go to extremes to recover an item of value. It is interesting that the stories are told together. The Lost Son story is third of the three. It begins with the words, "Jesus continued," perhaps to imply that if we spend so much effort to find one lost sheep and if we search the house from top to bottom for one lost coin, how much more should we spend on a human being that has gone missing?

In the Parable of the Lost Son, Jesus continued: "There was a man who had two sons. The younger one said to his father, 'Father, give me my share of the estate.' So he divided the property between them." The beginning of the story makes it clear the younger son was a scoundrel. He asked for his inheritance early—a request that would be an insult to his father. And then, look what happened. "Not long after that, the younger son got together all he had, set off for a distant country and there squandered his wealth in wild living." Not only did the younger son grab his share too soon, he squandered it—he was a wastrel, with nothing to commend him. Are there people in your life who are squandering their resources? I think of a young woman who started working at eighteen. She worked so hard for years, without taking adequate care of her body, that she is now in constant physical pain. If she doesn't get help she will not be able to support herself for the rest of her life. She is in her mid-twenties. What will she do for the rest of her days?

The Lost Son story establishes our value to God. We live in a strange world in which we assert our value in a context of such extreme freedom that we forget how dependent we are upon other people in order to survive and certainly to flourish. Our personal authenticity needs to be situated in a wider "horizon of meaning" than the little picture of what many of us think we want. For one thing, what we want at a particular time in our lives may cause harm and disorder down the road. Limits to human freedom are built into what it means to be human and not divine. We are the creatures of a "Chain of Being" (to use a medieval Christian concept) that acts back on us if we are foolish and too independent. The prodigal son was foolish and too independent. What about you? How do you balance your absolute value to God with your capacity to make good decisions about the action you should take to capitalize on your gifts and to stay close to a Loving Father?

*Lord Jesus, let me know that you find me when I am lost and love me no matter where I am now.*

# 27

# PARALYZING FEAR

*Luke 15:8-10*

Our mistakes can leave our lives in disarray. I think of a young man who was involved in sports throughout primary and secondary school. If he came off the field after an incident, his coaches would ask him: are you hurt or are you injured? If he said he was injured they would take him out of the game. He almost never told them the truth because he feared what it might cost the whole team. He would say he was hurt. He is now in graduate school. Due to these injuries, he lives in constant pain. He is in his mid-twenties. What is he going to do for the rest of his life?

I think of young women who excel in sports but persuade themselves that if they could just be lighter, thinner, they would be faster (a complete social-deception if you consider that muscle tissue is heavier than fat tissue). These women may end up with injury or anorexia and live with the lifelong outcome. I think of a young woman who lost an educational scholarship, endured the sorrow of abortion and dropped out of school. She was afraid she would lose her relationship if she did not go along with what her boyfriend wanted. She now has neither the boyfriend nor the education. She is so sad.

What happens when we make choices, the cost of which we did not count? How will these young people find new life? How will they hear God? Are you, were you one of them? I was. The story of the Lost Son continues: "After [the younger son] had spent everything, there was a severe famine in that whole country, and he began to be in need. So he went and hired himself out to a citizen of that country, who sent him to feed pigs. He longed to fill his stomach with the pods that the pigs were eating, but no-one gave him anything."

The consequences of foolish or misguided action leave emptiness in the human heart—we are more like a deserted lot than a beautiful garden. When we are young, we often fail to calculate the inevitable outcomes of choices we make. Yet there is nothing these young people have done that God would find surprising. God does not turn away because of what we do. God is used to this sort of thing. The parable of a young boy who ran away to enjoy radical freedom shows us that longing itself is a sign we are God's children. What are the longings in your own heart? What lies unsatisfied within the borders of your heart's garden? What grows there? Longing tells us that we have lost something we need. What do you do with your longings? Do you drown them out with mental chatter? Do you work yourself to exhaustion so they cannot be heard? Do you seek out substances that seem to silence your longings for a while, until you have to pay the price for a substitution that can never satisfy? What do you fear about the longings in your heart? Are they too big for you? Do you imagine they are too big, too hard for God? Are you angry? Is your fear that God will not or cannot forgive your sin, keeping you in bondage to it?

*Lord, there are places in the garden of my heart I never go because I have no idea what would happen to me if I went there. Release me, Lord. Comfort me. Show me that nothing is impossible for you. I am afraid of my self—of my passion, my desires. I am scared that you can't help me. What am I to do? Please come with me to those places. Show me that you are not afraid of them, or of me.*

*Lord Jesus Christ, lover of my soul—release me into your care so I can face you fully.*

# 28

# CITIZENS IN A FAR COUNTRY

*Luke 15:11-21*

Young men and women chase after extreme freedom and their losses are enormous. But we do not have to be young to be foolish.

There is a character in the story of the Lost Son that I never paid attention to before: the citizen in a far country. I wonder what would have happened if that citizen had been generous to the lost boy instead of merely providing a place to work and enough food to subsist on, but not to fill his stomach. The citizen, too, was affected by the famine. The boy began to starve.

Did the citizen remind him of home and its possibilities—opportunities open even to a prodigal? If we choose to be a citizen in a far country for someone else's children, how should we act? How do we provide a context for lost sons and daughters to feel the longings that remind them of home? What do prodigal children really need? What will we do for other people's children? Do we live in a culture that makes it so easy to leave home that runaways never have to face the consequences of their action? What is the famine in our social circumstances, particularly North America? What are we desperately short of? Do you sense the hunger of our age? What do you have to offer the hungry? In his compassion for those in need of food, Jesus said to the disciples: "You feed them." A few small loaves and fishes are sufficient, with God.

The Lost Son story also intrigues us if we want to know why there is no woman in it. I like to imagine what I would have been doing if I had been there. Of course…nothing would have been my fault! I wasn't the one who gave away the money and opened up the possibility for our son to get lost. When the son left for a far country, I would have said to the father something like: So what did you do that for? Why did you give him the money in the first place? Look what he did with it? You should have known not to give it to him! Look what happened! Why don't you go get him? Don't you care about my son? Why do you do nothing? Get him back? Do something! Where is he? If you loved him, if you loved me, you would do something!

Strange, isn't it. When we consider that the father in this story stands for God, we do talk to God this way. Often we are angry with God because someone we care about is not getting better. God endures our passion patiently as we pray for those we love—people in the middle of squandering their wealth. And we worry. We forget God is larger than our little backyard and has citizens in the far country where our children, husbands, siblings, friends, fathers and mothers wander. It is painful to ask: God what are you doing? But with the psalmist, we ask the question and await an answer. In the quiet stillness, gazing at an empty horizon, we wait like the father in this story, for the prodigal to come back home. And we ask for patience while we nervously search the horizon.

*Lord, I do ask for patience. Please let me not fear patience and distrust my own ability to figure out what to do while I am waiting. I also wait for you. Come and speak to me. Let me know you and hear your voice. Show me how this young man's father waited. Let me see it. Teach me to wait well. I don't like waiting. Help me understand that waiting is also a godly activity when you are in it. Please come and sit on the front steps and wait with me.*

*Lord Jesus Christ, have mercy.*

# 29

# COMING HOME

*Luke 15:22-31*

Finally the lost son saw that being a servant in his father's house was better than starving in a foreign field. He may have wasted his wealth but he did not squander his suffering. He let pain lead him home. "But while he was still a long way off, his father saw him and was filled with compassion for him; he ran to his son, threw his arms around him and kissed him. The son said to him, 'Father, I have sinned against heaven and against you. I am no longer worthy to be called your son.' But the father said to his servants, 'Quick! Bring the best robe and put it on him. Put a ring on his finger and sandals on his feet. Bring the fattened calf and kill it. Let's have a feast and celebrate. For this son of mine was dead and is alive again; he was lost and is found." So they began to celebrate. How do you come to your senses?

What has helped? Being in foreign field may not be literal. Perhaps we succumb to lies our culture tells about what makes life good. Coming to our senses is hard work. North America is famished for moral integrity. Perhaps your story is hard to tell due to sorrow, betrayal and disappointment. Coming to our senses, we return to a place we ran away from—often old wounds—a personal decision, sometimes made alone.

The younger son was driven home by necessity and by an idea of what makes life good. What is it that helps a child come to her senses? Wouldn't we like to know? Many of us suffer deeply as we watch someone we love misuse resources through debt, depression and despair. We don't know how to help. The story doesn't tell us what to do while we wait for someone to come to their senses—we must use imagination and wisdom. But we wait for the prodigals in our lives in such a way that we can express compassion for them when they do come home. We wait for prodigal beloved in a way that enables us to love them instantly, the moment they come to their senses, but also in a way that lets them do their own emotional work. We do not do it for them. That is why waiting well depends upon gardening our own hearts. We get on with farming our own land and leave our beloved to hard lessons learned far away. But while we wait for our own to return, we can be citizens in a far country for someone else's child.

Perhaps you protest my comparison between the lost son and current examples of the way young people squander their resources. Wait a minute, you say. Stories you tell of today are full of other people's sins. Girls are raped, impregnated by someone else, pornographers, television, media, and careless coaches—these people are to blame for the wasted years and pain you describe. You have a point. I do know Jesus said it would be better for someone who harms one of his little ones to have a mill stone tied around the neck and be thrown into the deepest part of the sea, than face God on Judgment Day. Yet isn't it interesting that the Lost Son is given no one but himself to blame for getting lost? In Jesus' day, people would have blamed the boy. Even so, the father forgives. Even if it was his own fault entirely, the father runs to meet him. That insight comforts me. Even if I am completely to blame for squandering my resources, God forgives and restores me. Can you accept God's grace for your foolishness? Are we willing to offer God's grace to other foolish people?

*Lord Jesus Christ, open my heart. Open my heart to my own human need for forgiveness. Help me forgive my self for being human and teach me to love the humanity you gave me as a gift. I will always be foolish unless you help me. I pray not just for my self. Open my heart to forgive those who have not given me what I needed.*

*Lord, have mercy.*

# 30

# ARE YOU ENVIOUS
# BECAUSE I AM GENEROUS?

*Matthew 20:1-16*

Jesus told a parable that depicts an inability to rejoice with those who rejoice. He described a scene in which a landlord invited various workers to till his fields; some began in the morning, some in the afternoon and some started just before closing time. At the end of the day, the landlord offered each worker the same reward. Those who worked longer were furious at what seemed to be an unfair distribution, even though it was what they agreed to in the morning and was very good pay. To their anger he responded: Are you envious because I am generous?

> "Meanwhile, the older son was in the field. When he came near the house, he heard music and dancing. So he called one of the servants and asked him what was going on. 'Your brother has come,' he replied, 'and your father has killed the fattened calf because he has him back safe and sound.'" The older brother became angry and refused to go in. So his father went out and pleaded with him. But he answered his father, 'Look! All these years I've been slaving for you and never disobeyed your orders. Yet you never gave me even a young goat so I could celebrate with my friends. But when this son of yours who has squandered your property with prostitutes comes home, you kill the fattened calf for him! 'My son,' the father said, 'you are always with me, and everything I have is yours. But we had to celebrate and be

glad, because this brother of yours was dead and is alive again; he was lost and is found.'"

You see there is simply nothing you can do to lose the love of God. You can even be grumpy with God. Whether you are the lost child or the elder child, God's love for you is certain. No mistake you make can sever you from the love of God. God will have it so. The courage to act, to turn the door-handles of our days, comes from the absolute assurance that God loves us regardless. Unlike many of us, the father in the parable let the son go and welcomed him back without inflicting guilt. Further, his love for the son who stayed was as certain as for the son who ran away. What is it like for the lost to be around you?

Suppose you lost a sheep, a coin or a son: what would you do? I want to reflect on the story of the Lost Son to ask about a fourth loss that women experience—we have lost our sisters and the sense of solidarity that kept women sane in the good old days. At least, solidarity kept us sane and safe, if the old days *were* good. As my mother used to say, but I didn't understand or appreciate it at the time, *if women would just be good to each other, the world would be a better place.* I suggest that, right now, the world is not a good or a safe place for our sisters, daughters or our selves. The reason in part is because we have not learned to be good to each other. Now the primary problem does not lie with the way women treat other women. As Mary Pipher said in *Reviving Ophelia*, we live in a girl-destroying culture. So I do not wish to blame women. Rather I want to consider how much better women's lives could be if we all enjoyed the love and support of other women. I would urge us to establish new pathways for women, from girlhood onwards, to learn to love their sisters and themselves. Let Jesus ask you often: Are you envious because I am generous with your sisters?

*Lord Jesus Christ, Child, Son, Savior and Lord, let me rest my desires in you. Garden my heart with me. Help me pull out weeds of envy that keep popping up and prevent me from rejoicing with those who rejoice. Show me how to love my sisters, with you.*

# EVERY EVENING
# HAS A BED IN IT
## DEVOTIONS 31-40

# 31

# EVERY EVENING
# HAS A BED IN IT

*Matthew 11:25-30*

If mornings have mirrors, and each day offers door-handles to turn, every evening has a bed in it. Beds are places to lay down our weary bones and unclutter chattery minds. In bed, we stretch out and feel support underneath. Recently, after coming back from staying in hotels, I lay down on my own bed and reflected on the privilege it is to have a bed of one's own. I was overcome with gratitude for a clean, sturdy, soft, safe place to rest and sleep. Many folk have no place to rest—for all sorts of reasons. Gardening the heart is a pre-requisite to finding rest as we lay on our own beds at night. It is one of the places we can do some of our gardening, if we tend the heart with the Holy Spirit's help.

Having a bed of one's own does not automatically mean that we can rest on it. Even if every evening has a bed in it, it is God's grace that enables us to find rest. After a long day's work, we seek rest. Rest is a gift from God. God offers rest to His children/friends. Our work is to garden our hearts so that the growth that nourishes our rest is beautiful and free of weeds. Weedy hearts are most troublesome when we are trying to get some rest. Gardening the heart is not laborious; but resting is an art. Finding rest in the heart's garden takes practice.

We do not find rest only in bed. The rest that God's grace offers can be taken into the waking world. Allowing our place of rest to fill our waking hours with stillness requires practice; it is a Christian spiritual discipline. In order to find rest we must leave behind the daily grind. Finding rest and leaving work are often linked. We must come to our senses in order to find rest. "When he came to his senses, [the younger son] said, 'How many of my father's hired servants have food to spare, and here I am starving to death! I will set out and go back to my father and say to him: Father, I have sinned against heaven and against you. I am no longer worthy to be called your son; make me like one of your hired servants.' So he got up and went to his father."

In Christ, there is eternal rest and daily rest. The second does not automatically follow the first. First of all, we do not rest while wandering in a far country, away from the Father. We only relax about eternal rest by coming home. And we find daily rest by asking two questions: What is my work? What is not my work? We find rest daily by doing our own proper, personal work in the daylight, rather than hiring our selves out to work with someone else's pigs. We find rest in the evening by letting go of work we cannot carry out at night. Finding rest requires learning to let other people do their own appropriate work, including God, and doing work God asks us to do while it is daylight. When we lay down to rest at night, we cannot be in two places at once, and must let go of the work that cannot be done in bed at night. But we can do some gardening.

*Lord Jesus Christ, have mercy on me. There are weeds in my garden. Help pull them out. Reveal them to me. I love to have them slip out easily, root and all. Show me the beauty flourishing in so many places in my heart. Water the growth with your presence. Let the river of life, that flows from the throne of God and the Lamb, nourish everything touched so that the trees in my garden will produce fruit in season for the feeding and the healing of all those who seek shelter under their leaves, including me, those closest to me and strangers sent from you. Thank you, Lord.*

# 32

# THIS SISTER OF YOURS

*Luke 10:38-42*

The elder child is unable to love the lost son as long as he says he is a wastrel. Did the elder brother change his mind? The invitation was offered. The elder son said to his father: This son of yours. The father replied: This brother of yours. In Genesis 4: 9-10, God said to Cain: Where is your brother? I don't know is the reply. Am I my brother's keeper? The Lord said: What have you done? Listen! Your brother's blood cries out to me from the ground. It is not just brothers who murder each other. Women sin against women. God loves women as much as God loves men—not more and not less. What about you? What is your opinion of other women? Are women your friends, colleagues, leaders and pastors? Do women love you as you exercise your gifts? I hope you can answer yes, but affirmation among women is not what I observe in general.

Women hold sexist views,[20] just as men do, since we all grow up in the same culture. Some women are hostile toward other women and do not like, trust, respect or find their statements to be credible. To the extent that women are oppressed, we have also internalized the prevailing misogynist ideology, which we uphold both in order to survive and in order to improve our own individual positions vis-à-vis other women. When they sin, men are aggressive in direct, physical and dramatic ways but women are aggressive in verbal and indirect ways. Women abuse indirectly by name-calling, insulting, teasing, threatening, shunning, isolating, becoming friends with another as a means of revenge, ignoring, gossiping, telling bad stories behind another person's back, and trying to get others to dislike that person. Cliques are the female equivalent of bullies—offering security to those who conform and insecurity in those who don't. Many women abuse, punish and hate the women their husbands are philandering with rather than the husbands themselves. Women who are hostile toward other women are not people of hope; they do not feel good about themselves. They have low self-esteem and have low life satisfaction when they are compared to women who are not hostile toward other women.

Many women won't support a woman leader. Some women unconsciously expect other women to mother them and feel betrayed when a woman fails to meet their ideal standards. Oddly, many women also have rather low standards for other women. Many are afraid to ask other women directly for what they want in order to avoid feeling shamed or disappointed when a friend refuses to stand by them through a life crisis. What keeps us from standing with each other?

I want women to treat each other more realistically and minimize unrealistic expectations, to bond together despite differences, experience disagreements less personally, hold grudges briefly not eternally, disagree without annihilating each other, be liberated from 'niceness' to telling the truth in love. What women do or refuse to do for one another matters deeply. Women have real power over each other that can be used consciously and ethically. We have power to encourage our sisters and need humility to receive that gift from other women. Change envy to compassion, betrayal to cooperation. The quiet, daily practice of sisterhood requires kindness, discipline and self-love. It also requires the capacity to respect rather than violate another woman's boundaries. Women that garden their own hearts can do this. Progress is daily.

*Lord Jesus, friend of women, have mercy. Let me see other women the way you see them, as friends. Lord have mercy on me.*

# 33

# RESTING ON THE PROMISES

*Jeremiah 29:11-14*

The pain we carry to our beds at night must be faced and examined. Where is the pain? What is it like? My niece is a massage therapist. She understands physical pain. We were talking once and she pointed out that pain is interesting. When she is in pain she pays attention to it and asks her self questions about it. She attends to the pain in her body by trying to specify exactly what kind of pain it is. Is it sharp pain? Is it a buzzing pain? Where is it exactly? As she observed it, she noticed that pain is always moving. I tried her experiment and she is right. If we think we are stuck in pain, it is much harder to bear. I wonder if emotional pain is very different?

Attending to the presence of pain-causing weeds is the heart's spiritual work. We have to name and know where the weeds are before we can pull them out. At least, that is our work most of the time. God does choose to remove weeds for us, miraculously. We wake up in the morning and realize that, without understanding why, we no longer feel anger towards a troublesome person that harried our hearts—forgiveness is a gift. This happens sometimes, as God wills. Most of the time, God cooperates with the effort we spend pulling out weeds so that we can find rest.

There are particular assurances that we need in order to find rest on our beds in the evening. We need to know we have a mission and a future. We need something to do each day and we need to sense that the future is good. It is our daily work to be citizens in a far country for lost daughters and sons. Women are Homemakers. Women who worked hard for the benefit of all women at the beginning of the twentieth century knew something that many of us have forgotten: we are here to make the world home for other people and for our selves.

For example, in 1910 suffragist Rheta Childe Dorr wrote that "a woman's place is in the Home, but Home is not contained within the four walls of an individual dwelling. Home is the community." If our future is secure because heaven is our true Home, we are free to create home on earth for others, in God's name. Creating home means encouraging hospitality, trust, safety, kindness, creativity and meaning. We encourage the presence of these humanizing elements of ordinary experience so they can play significant parts in our life together. We use leadership to grasp an opportunity to make life more humane. We use our circumstances to make the world more like a good home.

It is through God's grace we receive both assurances—of a mission and of a future. Receiving these tasks means that we have work to do. In these tasks, our spiritual responsibility is to discern what our work is and what God's work is. Resting in God evolves from addressing the distinction between our work and God's work. The discernment we need to develop takes time and requires wisdom. In James 1:5 we are promised that, "if any of you lacks wisdom, you should ask God, who gives generously to all without finding fault, and it will be given to you."

Finding rest requires wisdom for our daily work—our mission.

*Lord, I ask for wisdom and trust your promise that you give it generously, without finding fault with my foolishness and failures. Show me what you want me to do today. Send me friends and strangers that need to know of your love. Let me laugh and weep with them, for your sake. I know I am your hands, face and feet.*

# 34

# REALIZING GRACE

*John 15:9-17*

Perceiving that we have a good future comes through knowing the Word of God. In Jeremiah 31:1-14 we are given a vision of the future God has for all of us.

"At that time," declares the LORD, "I will be the God of all the families of Israel, and they shall be My people." Thus says the LORD, "The people who survived the sword found grace in the wilderness—Israel, when it went to find its rest." The LORD appeared to [them] from afar, saying, "I have loved you with an everlasting love; therefore I have drawn you with loving kindness. Again I will rebuild you, and you shall be rebuilt, O virgin of Israel! Again you shall take up your tambourines, and go forth to the dances of the merrymakers. Again you shall plant vineyards on the hills of Samaria; the planters shall plant and shall enjoy them. For there shall be a day when watchmen on the hills of Ephraim shall call out, Arise, and let us go up to Zion, to the LORD our God." For thus says the LORD, "Sing aloud with gladness for Jacob, and shout among the chiefs of the nations: proclaim, give praise, and say, 'O LORD, save Thy people, the remnant of Israel.' "Behold, I am bringing them from the north country, and I will gather them from the remote parts of the earth, among them is the blind and the lame, the woman with child and she who is in labor with child, together; a great company, they shall return here. "With weeping they shall come, and by supplication I will lead them; I will make them walk by streams of waters, on a straight path in which they shall not stumble; for I am a father to Israel. And Ephraim is my first-born." Hear the word of the LORD, O nations, and declare in the coast-lands afar off, and say, "He who scattered Israel will gather [them], and keep [them] as a shepherd keeps his flock." For the LORD has ransomed Jacob, and redeemed [them] from the hand of [those] who were stronger than [Israel]. "And they shall come and shout for joy on the height of Zion, and they shall be radiant over the bounty of the LORD—over the grain, and the new wine, and the oil, and over the young of the flock and the herd; and their life shall be like a watered garden, and they shall never languish again. Then the virgin shall rejoice in the dance, and the young men and the old, together, for I will turn their mourning into joy, and will comfort them, and give them joy for their sorrow. And I will fill the soul of the priests with abundance, and my people shall be satisfied with my goodness, declares the Lord."

Scripture unveils the beauty of God's grace for those who are his children and become his friends. In John chapters 14-17, Jesus reveals to the disciples that they are no longer God's servants but his friends. A servant doesn't know what the Master is doing; friends come to know God so well that they see patterns of godly activity that play out in the world. Friends recognize God. Through God's grace we are given a mission and a future as we come to see what God is like. Friends are satisfied with God's goodness and know that the world is in God's hands.

*Lord, let me be sure that you securely hold the world. It is not my work to hold up the world but simply to love it. I am your servant, I long to be your friend. I can hardly believe you want my friendship. But help me see that this is true. I have confused being God with being God's friend. I try to hold the world in my own hands, without trusting you. Thank you that you have the whole world in your hands. My future, my mission, my life is in your hands. I do trust you. Help me trust you more. Have mercy.*

# 35

# LIVING GRACE

*Revelation 3:20*

Friends can relax with each other. Our friendship with God is built on grace. We are told that grace and truth came through Jesus Christ: And the Word became flesh and lived among us, and we have seen his glory, the glory as of a father's only son, full of grace and truth (John 1:14). From Christ's fullness we have all received grace upon grace (John 1:16). Because of Jesus we know that we have all obtained access to God's grace in which we stand (Rom 5:2) so that sin will have no dominion over us, since we are not under law but under grace (Rom 6:14). And because of God we can all say: By the grace of God I am what I am, and his grace toward me has not been in vain (1 Cor 15:10). And even more than that, we can hear God say to us: "My grace is sufficient for you, for power is made perfect in weakness" (2 Cor 12:9). And this blessing rests upon us as we rest on our beds in the evening: In him we have redemption through his blood, the forgiveness of our trespasses, according to the riches of his grace (Eph 1:7) even when we were dead in our trespasses, we are made alive together with Christ—by grace you have been saved (Eph 2:5) so that in the ages to come he might show the immeasurable riches of his grace in kindness toward us in Christ Jesus (Eph 2:7).

There are door-handles in each day that we are alive. We have work to do: Therefore, prepare your minds for action; discipline yourselves; set all your hope on the grace that Jesus Christ will bring you when he is revealed in his glory (1 Pet 1:13). In times of difficulty, we remember that Scripture says: "After you have suffered for a little while, the God of all grace, who has called you to his eternal glory in Christ, will himself restore, support, strengthen, and establish you" (1 Pet 5: 10). May grace and peace be yours in abundance. And because of Christ, we have this perpetual blessing: "The grace of our Lord Jesus Christ, the love of God, and the communion of the Holy Spirit be with all of you" (2 Cor 13:13). In our beds at night, we rest on the promise of God's grace that is sufficient for all our needs and generous besides. Grace is related to faith and trust.

It is time that those of us who love God more than any other love took up a challenge that the world throws our way. We have work to do. When my children were little I became aware that if I gave them my undivided attention for a period of time, they were free and eager to move off my lap and engage with others in the world. I think God's lap is available to us for just the same reason. We rest with God and then we climb down and get to work. What is the most urgent work that we can take on right now? I offer the following description of social capital, or social trust, as an indication of what must be done. In my view, there is a desperate need for new programs for girls and women that will help us understand how we can create the safety and the challenges that women seek. When we get adequate rest on our beds every evening we have the emotional, spiritual and intellectual energy to change the world, for the Kingdom's sake.

*Lord I want to be a change agent in this world of yours. Let me see it as my world too. I spent some of my energy being angry, resentful, fearful and tired. I need your energy, which comes from friendship with you, to get to work and to find adequate and heart nourishing rest each day. Let me work and rest in you. Give me the wisdom to see the difference. I ask for your joy! I claim the promise that you are with us until the end of the age. Thank you for giving me your Spirit.*

# 36

# WHAT IS GRACE?

*Revelation 22:1-5*

Theologically, *grace* refers to God's unmerited favor. One manifestation of that definition is expressed in the acrostic GRACE = God's Riches at Christ's Expense. Through grace, we have life due to the purpose and plan of God, realized in the saving work of Jesus Christ in his death and his resurrection, and through the power of the Holy Spirit. Both aspects of Christ's life, his dying and his rising again, constitute our life in God's grace. Learning to die and learning to live are dimensions of resting in God. Grace makes dying and living possible and has other aspects that help us understand how to recognize and to live God' grace. Grace

- is a pleasing quality, it is attractive, charming and elegant,
- refers to elegant proportions, refinement of movement, action, expression or manner
- is becoming, or comely
- refers to being sufficiently conscious of duty and decency
- refers to social graces, attractive features, accomplishments or personal ornaments
- grace notes refer to the extra notes that embellish a harmony or melody, a musical surprise
- is a favor, benignant regard or its manifestation, from a superior
- if it refers to being in someone's good graces implies that we have someone's special favour
- refers to unconstrained good will
- is a privilege or concession that cannot be claimed as a right

- refers to God's favor
- unmerited favor of God, divine favor; regenerating, inspiring, strengthening influence
- refers to divinely given talent
- is the favor shown by granting a delay
- refers to the time allowed after a debt falls due
- refers to mercy, clemency
- refers to thanksgiving before a meal
- is a reference to the grace cup: a cup of wine passed around after grace is said.
- and a graceless person is unregenerate, depraved.

The offer of a bed to rest upon every evening comes from God. God gives us rest graciously. How is grace expressed in ordinary living? Grace

- is like a woman who teaches her husband how to love her in the way she needs to be loved
- is like a child who, having been disciplined unfairly, brings his mother a flower from the lawn
- is an embrace, a cosmic embrace, that one human being offers another on God's behalf
- is the time we give to reconcile a long-standing friendship that failed, surprising both people
- is trying again and again, seventy-times-seven, with someone who hurts us again and again
- is the welcome shock that God made you human, only human, and being human is good enough
- is the humbling surprise that God is pleased with you and that you are God's beloved
- is carried into the world by those who love God more than any other love
- climbs up on God's lap, lets her feet dangle, her muscles relax, and lays back on God's arm
- finds the secure, deep, eternal rest on the lap of a tirelessly loving God.

*Thank you, Lord.*

# 37

# WHAT DO YOU WANT GOD TO DO FOR YOU?

*Mark 10:35-45*

The joyful balance between working and resting, resting and working is possible when we let God know what we want. I say what we want not simply what we need. Human need is complex. We talk ourselves into needing many things that people in earlier times never dreamed of getting. In the consumer society of the early twenty-first century, human need is confusing. People have too much food; other people are starving. People have too much peace (peace at any price); other people have no peace at all. How does it help us to ask God for what we want?

Jesus takes care of what we want. His disciples, James and John, were brothers in a rich, elite family. They were accustomed to privilege. They approached Jesus and said: "We want you to do for us whatever we ask" (Mark 10:35). I have sometimes heard children make this request. The child wants commitment in advance: say yes before you know what I want, so you have to give it, no matter what it is. James and John imagined that they needed to trick Jesus to get what they wanted. Jesus was not fooled and could not be manipulated. What do you want me to do for you? They made their request: Let one of us sit at your right and the other at your left in your glory. Elite people see a need for elite positions. Their request made sense to them and to their family.

I have always found it easier to love those beneath me than those above me in the social order. My initial response is the same as the other disciples when they found out what the brothers asked for: they were indignant. But Jesus was not offended by the request of these two young men. He loved them. He loved them too much to give them what they thought they wanted. "Can you suffer what I suffer" he asked them. In their confidence they said yes. "Well," he replied, "You will drink the cup I drink and be baptized with my baptism. But as for who will sit on my right and left hand, that is not for me to say." Jesus saw the boundaries around what we can have. God is the one who maintains these limits, for our own good. What do you want?

Then there was blind Bartimaeus. He was sitting by the roadside begging. When he saw Jesus he began to shout: "Jesus, Son of David, have mercy on me!" This is the Jesus prayer. Bartimaeus cried out to the Lord for help and refused to be silenced or shut out by those around him. Jesus said to him: "What do you want me to do for you?" This is the same question he asked the two rich brothers. But this time, when the blind man asked for sight, Jesus gave it to him. What are we to learn from telling Jesus what we want? (Mark 10: 46-52)

We are wrong if we think Jesus loved blind people more than James and John. What we ask for is not the point. We must ask; even if we don't get it. We cannot understand our selves or God unless we sense what we want and come to God for it. God is not offended. God knows what we want before we say it aloud. Friendship is asking for what we want whether or not we get it. Being God's friend means we are free to ask. Granting our request is up to God. We ask for things and we have no idea what it would mean to have them. God says no. We ask for something miraculous and God says yes. It is our work to ask. We rest in God's wisdom to grant what he will to us. Our work is to grow wise in asking, by asking. We learn to trust God and to value our selves.

*Jesus, lover of my soul, let me hide in you. Help me offer the world mature love.*

# 38

# NEW RULES

*Matthew 26:36-46*

The times we are living in prize passion. We are to be moved by passion so that we become all we are meant to be. We think of passion positively. Sophie Freud, Sigmund's granddaughter, has a different view of passion.[21] She describes passion as an intense and obsessive emotion. Passion is a preoccupation with and a yearning for a love object that involves or does not involve sexual desire. Passion's root word conveys its relationship to suffering. Passion is a dark and irrational force that moves us to want something or someone despite conditions that surround that desire—conditions that are often obvious to other people but not to those enmeshed in passionate desire. Relentless, unquenchable wanting awakened by passion was called concupiscence in medieval language. Limitless wanting was one of the seven deadly sins. Sins were "deadly" because they led to spiritual despair. Hope, not despair, is our Christian heritage and our spiritual companion.

Passion involves anguish, doubts and uncertainty. Unrequited passion can turn into dejection and then despair. Two aspects of passion Sophie Freud points out: The passion experience is a wish for fusion of the self with another that over-evaluates the love object. The feelings of wanting to be one with another and to value the love-object above all consideration for one's self, lead on a downward spiral emotionally, physically and spiritually. The loss of one's own value in the passion experience encourages people to disregard their own needs, their own boundaries and the boundaries that should rightly surround the person or thing that passion drives us toward. The object of passion may be another adult, a possession, or our own children. Freud acknowledged that she was passionate about her first born son, not in a sexual sense, but in a sense that trapped them both in an unending and unsatisfying relationship. Neither of them flourished under these conditions. Passion in this sense is obsessive; it is a frightening and an exhilarating loss of and grasping for control. Control is the central aim. Passionate experience can prove to be beneficial to our lives if we move out of the experience and look back at it from a distance: it is good for us if we get over it. Passionate experience in the sense Sophie Freud explores is not mature love.

I agree with her that mature love exists when and only when the satisfactions and security of the loved person are approximately as important as one's own. In mature love, there is a balance between the lover and the loved one so that both people have relatively equal importance in the relationship. This is true in our relationship with God. It is not God's aim to erase human value.

In Christianity, all love has limits. In the New Testament we see a pattern that required believers to begin to think for themselves about how they should live. The old Jewish order was primarily a rule-governed religion. Jesus introduced a pattern that was to be lived from the inside out, not the outside in. As a result, we have to think about what we are doing; simply following the rules laid out by our community is not sufficient for mature faith. But there are rules. It is as if we rely on the rules when passion begins to get out of hand—even passion to do good—carried out at the expense of other people around us. How is your love life? Do you love too much or too little? Are there frightening love experiences that have shaped your hope in God? What has gone well?

*Lord Jesus Christ, Lover of my soul, have mercy on me. Help me focus on what I have done well in loving my self and others. I want to love my self and other people as you do. I need your help.*

# 39

# A NEW TESTAMENT PATTERN

*Acts 10:9-16*

As Jesus introduced a new order, initiated in the heart, the old order had to be reconceived. There are two ways, neither very helpful, to make a deep change. One is to be hateful towards old ways and the other is to be hard-lined with respect to a new way, latching on with a grip that stifles its growth and severs it from its roots. If the first response is modeled on hatred the second is tense with fear. Jesus was neither hateful nor fearful. How can we focus on Christian living from the heart so that we are given over to love and hope through trusting the Lord Jesus Christ? What boundary marks off the task to garden our hearts for God's sake, by the Holy Spirit's power, and by following Jesus' example? How may we learn to love God more than any other love?

Christians have to think in order to be faithful. Christianity is remarkable among world religions for its requirement that believers must work some things out, in concert with God and each other. Christianity is characterized by diversity that surrounds a common core of beliefs and practices that give faith its identity. And there is a pattern in Scripture that applies to gardening the heart.

The first disciples had to figure things out on the basis of Jesus' words and example. Peter, for one, had an experience during which he saw a sheet let down from heaven on which were all kinds of animals that Peter had been raised to avoid as food. Three times the sheet was let down. Three times a voice invited him to eat.

He refused because it would have broken his well-learned rules to do so. As he was reflecting on what God was conveying to him, servants from Cornelius, a god-fearing Gentile, came to his door to invite him to visit their master. Peter went. For the first time in his life he entered a gentile household. He did so because of his vision from God. As a consequence, the gentile world was introduced to Jesus.

Years ago I was meditating on that passage at the Banff Springs Hotel in Banff, Alberta. As I was walking down the hallway, back to my room, focused on what God requires of us, I saw a vision. I remember being so surprised that I stumbled against the hallway wall. The impression was of a sheet let down from heaven and a voice nudging me to see that there was a woman on that sheet. The voice echoed what was said to Peter: Do not call anything impure that God has made clean (Acts 10:15). That moment shifted by perception of my self and all other women, who I came to see as my people. Sometimes God requires a deep change in the depth of our hearts.

As the early Church was working out a relationship to God through Jesus Christ, rules to apply to believers were revised from the former Jewish system. The story of that transition begins in Acts 10 and Acts 15 and is elaborated in the rest of Scripture. The outcome of rethinking the rules was an emphasis on three principles: flee idolatry, flee sexual immorality and avoid relational harm. The principle of avoiding harm to others was eventually infused by a call to be a community of love, modeled on Christ's example, so that the third principle was expressed positively. Christ is the culmination of the old order so there is righteousness for everyone who believes (Rom 10). In Revelation we note that these three principles are employed in judgment (Rev 9:20-21). They are serious. We use them as tools to garden our hearts. What are your idols? Is sexual immorality in your life? Are you free to love others?

*Lord Jesus Christ, beautiful Savior, have mercy on me.*

# 40

# MULTIPLY PICNICS!

*Ephesians 2:11-22*

Due to my vocation, I live far away from my extended family. The times I miss them the most is when I see families gathered together, having a picnic in the park.

The church is a strange collection of people who are strangers to each other. We sometimes say we are a family but I don't think that quite captures what it means to be church. It is astonishing to consider that early church communities united slaves and free people, men and women, Jews and Gentiles. Their unity was unheard of and became a sign of God's divine presence—a witness to Christ's love and resurrection for all who saw how they behaved. They worked at community.

The work of being church is the toil involved in learning to love people that don't make sense to us. This side of heaven, it is work and not a simple pleasure. At a conference recently, I wanted to ask how many of the women there had been hurt in the church. I didn't ask. I wonder what they would have reported. I know what I would have said.

It is easy to idealize my family when I am far away. But I remember that people get hurt, even at picnics. Some kids are left out of the game. Some people eat too much. Some people get all the presents if it is a birthday party; some are shamed, just for being who they are. We feel afraid of an aunt or uncle, or jealous of a cousin who seems to be center-stage. Families can be unjust. The events at family picnics leave an impression on the heart. But I still feel sad riding my bike past a family picnic where it sure seems that they are having fun. Relational suffering is not worse than being all alone. Without God, people are all alone in the universe. And God comes with a family.

Garden your heart for God's sake. Pull out the weeds that accumulate because you have spent your life with people that make no sense to you, for whom, you seem to make no sense. Your heart's garden is a place of beauty and rest where you meet the Savior of the world, who loves you absolutely, generously and to the end. The weeds in our garden may be there because of injustice: pull them out! Free yourself so that you can get up in the morning; go out into the world and love it in Christ's name. That is your proper work. While it sometimes seems to us that the world needs to be chastened, it is in God's best interests to see that it needs to be loved, not in a servile fashion, as though you go through life always asking for a favor. You are God's beloved. Christ died, for you. You have nothing to feel ashamed about, certainly not your humanity, which is a gift from God. The weeds in your garden may be there due to your own foolishness: pull them out! You can do this with the help of the Holy Spirit. With God, nothing is impossible. But there is a catch. You have to want to be well and weed-free. Let go of what you think are the advantages that come to you from being grumpy or sad. Let God have your heart.

*Lord Jesus Christ, Lover of my soul, Gardener of hearts, let the adventure begin. Show me what you can do with me when I let you walk through the garden of my heart. Let me know that you are pleased with me and that I do many things that make you glad. I want my life to provide a safe haven for others to come and find rest. I want to know that I am safe with you. I am not yet sure what you will do with me, but I trust you, help me have more trust.*

*Lord, Jesus, have mercy.*

# NOTES

1. Sophie Freud, *My Three Mothers and Other Passions* (New York: New York University Press, 1991), 245-246.

2. Ana-Maria Rizzuto, *The Birth of the Living God* (Chicago: Chicago University Press, 1979), 187.

3. Ellen T. Charry, *By the Renewing of Your Minds* (New York: Oxford University Press, 1997), 64-65.

4. Sigmund Freud, *Totem and Taboo* (New York: Vntage Books, 1996), 98-129.

5. Anthony M. Coniaris, *Philokalia: The Bible of Orthodox Spirituality* (Minneapolis: Light and Life Publishing, 1998), 191.

6. Coniaris, 217.

7. Coniaris, 242.

8. Courtney Wilson, in a final paper written for CM 1EO3 on the topic of empowerment, April, 2003. McMaster Divinity College, Hamilton Ontario, 9. Used with permission.

9. Mary Pipher, *Reviving Ophelia* (New York: Ballantine Books, 1994).

10. Coniaris, 11.

11. Coniaris, 11.

12. Coniaris, 11.

13. Coniaris, 98-99.

14. Coniaris, 99-100.

15. Coniaris, 206.

16. "Police investigate bully girl in boy's death," reported in the *Hamilton Spectator* D3, April 13, 2002.

17 Charles Taylor, *The Ethics of Authenticity* (Cambridge Massachusetts: Harvard University Press, 1991), 78.

18. Collin Morris, *The Discovery of the Individual 1050-1200* (Toronto: University of Toronto Press, 2000), 44-45.

19. D.W. Winnicott, *Playing and Reality* (London: Tavistock, 1971), 10.

20. The following insights about women are taken from newspaper and magazine articles, personal experience, and two very significant new books:

Phyllis Chesler, *Woman's Inhumanity to Woman* (New York: Thunder's Mouth Press/Nation Books, 2001), 1-34; and *Dropped Threads,* edited by Carol Shields and Marjorie Anderson (Toronto: Vintage Canada, 2001).

21. Sophie Freud, 32-69.

Printed in the United States
30926LVS00003B/16-18

9 781894 667777